FIRST THINGS FIRST

[WHAT EVERY CHRISTIAN SHOULD KNOW]

Pastor Steve Morgan

ISBN-13: 978-0692638729
ISBN-10: 0692638725

BISAC: Religion / Christian Education / General

TABLE OF CONTENTS

FORWARD .... *III*

ACKNOWLEDGMENTS .... *V*

MY TESTIMONY .... *VII*

INTRODUCTION .... *IX*

BOOKS IN THE BIBLE LEGEND .... *XI*

BOOKS IN THE BIBLE .... *XII*

FIRST THINGS FIRST ~ SALVATION ~ *1*

WHAT DOES THE BIBLE SAY ABOUT SALVATION? 1
WHY DID JESUS HAVE TO DIE ON THE CROSS? 5
SALVATION SUMMARY 12
RECEIVING FORGIVENESS & FORGIVING 13
THERE ARE SOME OBLIGATIONS YOU HAVE TOWARDS GOD 21
THE PRINCIPLES OF LIFE & DEATH 23
SEPARATE YOURSELF 27
GRACE: UNMERITED FAVOR 31
MERCY: GETTING BETTER THAN YOU DESERVE 40
THE MINISTRY OF RECONCILIATION 43
WHEN THINGS GO WRONG 45
DEALING WITH OUR ISSUES 48
FASTING 52
THE BATTLEGROUND OF THE MIND 56
GOD CORRECTS THOSE WHOM HE LOVES 58
MONEY; GOD'S WAY 61
THE KING'S REPUTATION IS AT STAKE! 83
GOD WANTS TO USE YOUR TALENTS 87

WITNESSING *90*

LEARNING HOW TO LEARN *94*

COME UNTO ME 96
HERE A LITTLE, THERE A LITTLE 99
SHOW, TEACH, THEN DO 104

FROM THOUGHT TO DEED *106*

ANOTHER BLESSING FOR YOU *112*

WHAT'S NEXT? *118*

MORE OF MY PERSONAL TESTAMONIES *120*

FORWARD

Christianity really isn't hard. We make it hard because of our misconceptions. I made it hard on myself because I didn't know what the bible says about this lifestyle. That is why I wrote this book; to help others avoid the same challenges I went through.

If you want to know what Christianity is all about, this book is for you. I was finishing my first book (God's Blueprint for Spiritual Growth and Reward) when it dawned on me that I started in the middle of things. Being a linear person, I knew I couldn't just let things lie, so here it is; First Things First.

You may ask, what is the first thing that should take place as someone pursues a relationship with God through Jesus Christ? The bible clearly tells us what we should be learning first. This book starts from the beginning and builds upon each principle to help every Christian have a sure foundation according to the bible.

My plan is to start from the very beginning. I will be sharing principles in an order that will help you avoid some of the challenges I faced due to ignorance as a new born again believer.

ACKNOWLEDGMENTS

I have eternal gratitude to my Lord Jesus Christ who is my all in all. To my wife Georgette, who has always supported me in my endeavors; you are my queen. To my daughter Kiliea and son Michael Jr., whom I love very much; my greatest gift to you is what the Lord Jesus Christ has taught me.

There have been some significant men and women of God in my life. This book is possible because of their love, demonstration of Godliness and scriptural knowledge.
:

- Apostle B. R. Hicks ~ Christ Gospel International, Jeffersonville, Indiana. A mighty woman of God who poured a deep foundation in my life. Thank you for your Labor of Love.

- Bishop Anthony and Pastor Kelly McMillan ~ Pensacola Life Church, Pensacola, Florida. Thank you for your support, encouragement and love; you have become a pillar in my life.

- Apostle Nate and Pastor Valerie Holcomb ~ Christian House of Prayer, Killeen, Texas. Thank you for your ministry, insight, wisdom, understanding and patience.

- My current Pastor, Chris and Nikki Mathis ~ The Summit Church, Crestview, Florida. You have been the Balm of Gilead for my wife and I after a rough work; thank you.

Thanks to the saints in the bible study in Afghanistan who allowed me to use them as a sounding board for clarity while writing this book.

Special thanks to a friend, who wishes to remain anonymous, for proof reading my writings; the Lord used our discussions to help me put some of these principles into words. You are such a blessing and integral to the success of this book.

To my sister Candis, who helped me create the book cover... Cha Ching Ching.

MY TESTIMONY

My parents were not avid church goers. In fact, the main moral guidance given as I was a teenager was that I would be in serious trouble if I got any one pregnant.

I thought I was a nice guy. Looking back now, I am confident that I was a nice guy sinner going straight to hell.

In 1979, while stationed at Anderson Air Force Base Guam, I joined the base swim team. On our way to Saipan for an ocean swim meet, one of my team mates sat next to me on the plane. He showed me what the word of God says concerning salvation and asked me if I wanted to ask Jesus in to my heart. I declined then. He was sixteen years old, I was nineteen. I know now that God used him to plant the seed. I don't remember his name and have always wanted to thank him.

Fast forwarding a little, January 1982, Fort Walton Beach, Florida, I decided that I would like to get married and settle down. I thought it best to marry a woman who knows God. My father was difficult to live with and there was a chance that I would be as well. So my wife would probably need to call on a higher power from time to time. There was no way I could ask something of my spouse that I wouldn't do. So I thought to myself that I would accept all invitations to church for the next two weeks. I received seven invitations during those two weeks; none before or after. Oddly enough, I didn't consider this to be strange.

I began my quest to go to each of these churches every Sunday. I didn't know anything about what church should be like, so the different worship styles didn't bother me. I went to Baptist, Methodist, Charismatic, Non-Denominational,

Episcopal, Pentecostal and Catholic services; not necessarily in that order. However, at the last church I visited, May 2, 1982, Jesus came into my heart so powerfully that all my agendas melted away. At that point, all I wanted was to preserve this thing that I knew I had received; Jesus! I forgot about finding a wife and basked in the glory of His salvation, word and love.

Once saved, I no longer gave my daily guitar practice any time. I didn't know much, but I wasn't going to do anything that would affect my relationship with Jesus in a negative way; I put away my guitar for a season. Later I learned that He wanted my talent and I gave it to him with all my heart.

I stopped looking for a wife because I realized what I was really looking for was Jesus Christ. He filled the gaping void in my heart so completely that I was content to stay right where I was to get more of Him. To this day, I am so grateful that Jesus Christ came into my heart. I don't know what my fate would have been had he not saved me. I will forever be in debt to Jesus Christ and for that; I give my life to Him. Thank You Jesus!

Oh, and on the wife search… well, you'll just have to read on to find out about that miracle.

INTRODUCTION

Every subject mentioned in this book can easily be expounded upon to create its own book. My objective is to help you start a foundation that you can build upon that will never be shaken. I encourage you to return to these subjects and dig deeper after you have grasped these basic concepts.

First things First, if you want a relationship with God, then you need Jesus! You obtain Him by asking for forgiveness for your sins and asking Him to come into your heart to be your Lord and Savior. At this point you are "saved" from sin and death.

Your next step is to learn about the grace of God. Grace that helps you move forward in your walk with Jesus. You must study to understand grace so that you can continue to walk with Jesus, free from condemnation; even though you don't get it right all the time.

Learning of God's mercy will bring you to a place of gratitude. You will realize that you don't deserve it, and that the Lord Jesus Christ simply forgave you through His sacrifice. Jesus did all of this so that you wouldn't have to pay the price for your sin.

Proverbs 2:21 For the upright shall dwell in the land, and the perfect shall remain in it.

To be perfect you must stay under the grace of God. To do that you must learn more of His provisions for you

.

~The Author~

Pray with me:

Lord, cover me with your blood. Forgive me of my sins; known and unknown. Open my eyes of understanding. Let me see your word from your perspective and not mine. In Jesus' name I pray, Amen.

BOOKS IN THE BIBLE LEGEND

(Alphabetical, OT = Old Testament, NT = New Testament)

Acts ~ Acts (NT)	Jude ~ Jude (NT)
Amos ~ Amos (OT)	1 Kin ~ 1st Kings (OT)
1 Chr ~ 1st Chronicles (OT)	2 Kin ~ 2nd Kings (OT)
2 Chr ~ 2nd Chronicles (OT)	Lam ~ Lamentations (OT)
Col ~ Colossians (NT)	Lev ~ Leviticus (OT)
1 Cor ~ 1st Corinthians (NT)	Luke ~ Luke (NT)
2 Cor ~ 2nd Corinthians (NT)	Mal ~ Malachi (OT)
Dan ~ Daniel (OT)	Mic ~ Micah (OT)
Deu ~ Deuteronomy (OT)	Mark ~ Mark (NT)
Ecc ~ Ecclesiastes (OT)	Matt ~ Matthew (NT)
Eph ~ Ephesians (NT)	Nah ~ Nahum (OT)
Est ~ Esther (OT)	Neh ~ Nehemiah (OT)
Ex ~ Exodus (OT)	Num ~ Numbers (OT)
Eze ~ Ezekiel	Oba ~ Obadiah (OT)
Ezra ~ Ezra (OT)	1 Pet ~ 1st Peter (NT)
Gal ~ Galatians (NT)	2 Pet ~ 2nd Peter (NT)
Gen ~ Genesis (OT)	Phm ~ Philemon (NT)
Hab ~ Habakkuk (OT)	Php ~ Philippians (NT)
Hag ~ Haggai (OT)	Prov ~ Proverbs (OT)
Heb ~ Hebrews (NT)	Ps ~ Psalms (OT)
Hos ~ Hosea (OT)	Rev ~ Revelations (NT)
Isa ~ Isaiah (OT)	Rom ~ Romans (NT)
Jas ~ James (NT)	Ruth ~ Ruth (OT)
Jer ~ Jeremiah (OT)	1 Sam ~ 1st Samuel (OT)
Job ~ Job (OT)	2 Sam ~ 2nd Samuel (OT)
Joel ~ Joel (OT)	Son ~ Song of Solomon (OT)
John ~ John (NT)	1 Thes ~ 1st Thessalonians (NT)
1 Joh ~ 1st John (NT)	2 Thes ~ 2nd Thessalonians (NT)
2 Joh ~ 2nd John (NT)	1 Ti m~ 1st Timothy (NT)
3 Joh ~ 3rd John (NT)	2 Tim ~ 2nd Timothy (NT)
Jona ~ Jonah (OT)	Tit ~ Titus (NT)
Jos ~ Joshua (OT)	Zec ~ Zechariah (OT)
Jud ~ Judges (OT)	Zep ~ Zephaniah (OT)

BOOKS IN THE BIBLE

(In Order As Found In The Bible)

Old Testament (OT)	New Testament (NT)
Genesis ~ Gen	Nahum ~ Nah
Exodus ~ Ex	Habakkuk ~ Hab
Leviticus ~ Lev	Zephaniah ~ Zep
Numbers ~ Num	Haggai ~ Hag
Deuteronomy ~ Deu	Zechariah ~ Zec
Joshua ~ Jos	Malachi ~ Mal

Old Testament (OT)

Genesis ~ Gen
Exodus ~ Ex
Leviticus ~ Lev
Numbers ~ Num
Deuteronomy ~ Deu
Joshua ~ Jos
Judges ~ Jud
Ruth ~ Ruth
1st Samuel ~ 1Sam
2nd Samuel ~ 2Sam
1st Kings ~ 1Kin
2nd Kings ~ 2Kin
1st Chronicles ~ 1Chr
2nd Chronicles ~ 2Chr
Ezra ~ Ezra
Nehemiah ~ Neh
Esther ~ Est
Job ~ Job
Psalms ~ Ps
Proverbs ~ Prov
Ecclesiastes ~ Ecc
Song of Solomon ~ Son
Isaiah ~ Isa
Jeremiah ~ Jer
Lamentations ~ Lam
Ezekiel ~ Eze
Daniel ~ Dan
Hosea ~ Hos
Joel ~ Joel
Amos ~ Amos
Obadiah ~ Oba
Jonah ~ Jona
Micah ~ Mic

Nahum ~ Nah
Habakkuk ~ Hab
Zephaniah ~ Zep
Haggai ~ Hag
Zechariah ~ Zec
Malachi ~ Mal

New Testament (NT)

Matthew ~ Matt
Mark ~ Mark
Luke ~ Luke
John ~ John
Acts ~ Acts
Romans ~ Rom
1st Corinthians ~ 1Cor
2nd Corinthians ~ 2Cor
Galatians ~ Gal
Ephesians ~ Eph
Philippians ~ Php
Colossians ~ Col
1st Thessalonians ~ 1Thes
2nd Thessalonians ~ 2Thes
1st Timothy ~ 1Tim
2nd Timothy ~ 2Tim
Titus ~ Tit
Philemon ~ Phm
Hebrews ~ Heb
James ~ Jas
1st Peter ~ 1Pet
2nd Peter ~ 2Pet
1st John ~ 1Joh
2nd John ~ 2Joh
3rd John ~ 3Joh
Jude ~ Jude
Revelations ~ Rev

All scripture references will be from the Old King James Version translated in 1618 unless otherwise stated.

1

FIRST THINGS FIRST
~ SALVATION ~

It would be remiss of me to omit the very first step in a relationship with Jesus Christ. Without this step, the rest of this book is a wasted read.

Has anyone ever told you that God loves you and that He has a wonderful plan for your life?

I have a real quick, but important question to ask you. God forbid, but if you were to die this second, do you know for sure, beyond a shadow of a doubt, that you would go to Heaven?

Let me quickly share with you what the Holy Bible relays. It reads *"for all have sinned and come short of the glory of God (Romans 3:23)"* and *"for the wages of sin is death, but the gift of God is eternal life through Jesus Christ our Lord (Romans 6:23)"*. The Bible also reads, *"For whosoever shall call upon the name of the Lord shall be saved (Romans 10:13)"*. Would you say that you and I are a "whosoever"? Of course we are; all of us are.

If you would like to receive the gift God has for you today, say this prayer with your heart and voice out loud.

> Dear Lord Jesus, come into my heart, forgive me of my sin. Wash me and cleanse me. Set me Free. Jesus, I thank You that You died for me. I believe that You are the son of God, you died on the cross for my sins and that you rose from the dead to set me free. Fill me with the Holy Ghost. Give me a passion for the lost, a hunger for the things of God, and a holy boldness, to preach the gospel of Jesus Christ. In Jesus' name I pray, Amen.

Now you can say "I'm Saved: I'm born again, I'm forgiven, and I'm on my way to Heaven, because I have Jesus in my heart!"

As a minister of the gospel of Jesus Christ, I tell you today that all of your sins are forgiven. Always remember to **run to God** and not from Him because He loves you and has a great plan for your life.

Welcome to the family of God!

God has made it clear what constitutes salvation. Receiving salvation, entering into the kingdom of heaven, receiving Christ in your heart, and being born again are phrases that the Christian community uses to define joining the Family of God; they're synonymous. God's word is the measuring stick by which we will be judged on the Day of Judgment. So let's look at what the Bible says about this subject.

1.1

What Does The Bible Say About Salvation?

Luke 19:10 For the Son of man (Jesus) is come to seek and to save that which was lost.

Jesus came for you! He is waiting for you to surrender to His Loving Kindness.

2 Peter (2Pet) 3:9 ¶ The Lord is not slack concerning his promise, as some men count slackness; but is longsuffering to us-ward, **not willing that any should perish**, but that all should come to **repentance**.

It's clear that God's motive is to allow **all** of mankind to be saved. Some people believe that "they are too far gone to be saved". But God specializes in saving the lost and in his eyes; you're either saved or lost, there is no degree of lost that he cannot reach.

The Greek word for **Repentance** in 2Pet 3:9 is μετανοια, metanoia (pronounced met-an'-oy-ah); which means a change of mind, to change one's mind for better, heartily to amend with abhorrence of one's past sins. Once we repent, we receive salvation; our past sins are amended with God.

John 3:16 For God so loved the world, that he gave his only begotten Son, that whosoever **believeth** in him should not perish, but have everlasting life. **17** For God sent not his Son into the world to condemn the world; but that the world through him might be saved. **18** He that believeth on him is not condemned: but he that **believeth** not is condemned already, because he hath not believed in the name of the only begotten Son of God.

The Greek word for **Believeth** is πιστευω pisteuo (pronounced pist-yoo'-o); which means to commit to, commit to (one's) trust, be committed to, place confidence in, think to be true, and believer.

When we believe in Jesus Christ as the Son of God who died on the cross and was raised again the third day for us, we have taken the very first step into a life filled with a presence of God known only to his born again believers. And we have the blessed experience to be able to place our trust in His caring for our natural and spiritual needs.

Yes, Jesus will manifest in a wonderful way to take care of your natural needs as well as your spiritual needs if you place your trust in Him!

More on Salvation:

Romans (Rom) 10:9 That if thou shalt confess with thy mouth the Lord Jesus, and shalt believe in thine heart that God hath raised him from the dead, thou shalt be saved. **10** For with the heart man believeth unto righteousness; and with the mouth confession is made unto salvation. **11** For the scripture saith, Whosoever believeth on him shall not be ashamed.

Here is another prayer that brings a person and Jesus together. Say this prayer with your voice.

Lord Jesus I confess with my mouth that you are the Son of God and I believe in my heart that God has raised you from the dead. Forgive me of my sins. Come into my heart and be my Lord and Savior. Thank you for answering my prayer. In Jesus Name I pray. Amen.

Congratulations! It's as simple as that. If you prayed this prayer with a sincere heart, you are "born again". Welcome to the Kingdom of Heaven. Your Eternal Life starts now.

Remember!!!

Rom 10:13 For whosoever shall call upon the name of the Lord shall be saved.

So as you continue in this newness of life, call upon Jesus as often as possible!

Now that you have taken the first step of walking with Jesus, He wants you to know some things to protect you from harm. The rest of this book is about what every Christian should know. There are many stages and depths to each subject presented in this book. However, I will only be scratching the surface to help you quickly lay a foundation on which to build your destiny with Christ.

This is an exciting and rewarding journey; so hold on!

MY TESTAMONY

In the beginning of 1982, I started thinking about getting married. So I thought about what kind of wife I wanted. I wanted to make sure that we stayed married. I realized that might be a challenge as my dad was difficult with my mom. I figured the apple doesn't fall far from the tree so she would need to call on a higher power from time to time. I reasoned that she would need to be a Christian. Due to my issues with my dad telling me to do one thing and him doing another, I thought I would lead by example and go to church. Besides, where can you find a Christian wife? In the church of course!

Let me interject here that I grew up in a family that the main moral guidance was that I could not get anyone pregnant. So religion was somewhat foreign to me.

I came to the decision that for the next two weeks, I would accept any invitation to church. In those two weeks, I received seven invitations; none before and none after. For some reason, at the time, that didn't seem strange. All seven invitations were to different churches. So for the next seven Sundays, I went to each of the churches. I can't think of any denomination that was missed.

Finally, I went to the last church on my schedule. May 2, 1982. I sat in the back as I normally did. Ralph Washington, the usher, asked me to join him in the isle to dance before the Lord. I wanted to say no. But the next thing I knew, I was in the isle.   Right there Jesus touched me so wonderfully, that I forgot what I had come for (to find a wife). THIS WAS IT! I had found what I was really in need of. Jesus filled the gaping void in my heart.   I was so overwhelmed that I became desperate to keep this new found relief.

So I attended church every Sunday. I wanted more and was angry when I found out about Wednesday and Friday night services because several weeks had passed. My original plan to find a wife was gone and all I cared about was Christ.

I asked Jesus into my heart and I am so glad I did. I have done nothing to earn His love. Yet he gave it to me. If he will do this for me, then I know he will do it for you.

Thank you Jesus!

1.2

Why Did Jesus Have To Die On The Cross?

Throughout the Old Testament you will read about sacrifices, gifts and offerings made in the tabernacle or temple of God. This blood was shed in the morning and evening every day with the addition of special offerings in order to atone for the sins of the people and the priests. It was a bloody mess! This system was sufficient until the appointed time when God sent his only begotten Son to shed His perfect blood once and for all. You see animal blood could not fully atone for the sins of man. This is why the sacrifices were so often and each sacrifice was designed for a specific purpose. The system worked, but it was inadequate to do the job completely; it could not purge our conscience. God did not design the human body to harbor a guilty conscience so the system of that time needed to be reformed.

Hebrews (Heb) 9:1 ¶ Then verily the first covenant had also ordinances of divine service, and a worldly sanctuary. **2** For there was a tabernacle made; the first, wherein was the candlestick, and the table, and the shewbread; which is called the sanctuary. **3** And after the second veil, the tabernacle which is called the Holiest of all; **4** Which had the golden censer, and the ark of the covenant overlaid round about with gold, wherein was the golden pot that had manna, and Aaron's rod that budded, and the tables of the covenant; **5** And over it the cherubims of glory shadowing the mercyseat; of which we cannot now speak particularly. **6** Now when these things were thus ordained, the priests went always into the first tabernacle, accomplishing the service of God. **7** But into the second went the high priest alone once every year, not without blood, which he offered for himself, and for the errors of the people: **8 ¶** The Holy Ghost this signifying, that the way into the holiest of all was not yet made manifest, while as the first tabernacle was yet standing: **9 Which was a figure for the time then present, in which were offered both gifts and sacrifices, that could not make him that did the service perfect, as pertaining to the conscience; 10** Which stood only in meats and drinks, and divers washings, and carnal ordinances, imposed on them until the time of reformation. **11 But Christ being come an high priest of good things to come, by a greater and more perfect tabernacle, not made with hands, that is to say, not of this building; 12 Neither by the blood of goats and calves, but by his own blood he entered in once into the holy place, having obtained eternal redemption for us. 13** For if the blood of bulls and of goats, and the ashes of an heifer sprinkling the unclean, sanctifieth to the purifying of the flesh: **14 How much more shall the blood of Christ, who through the eternal Spirit offered himself without spot to God, purge your conscience from dead works to serve the living God?**

These passages tell of a process that maintained man's relationship with God. However, this was a temporary fix. God sent Jesus complete the cleansing process that would effectively purge our guilty conscience. Jesus was born of a virgin so that He would be man and God (Emmanuel, which means God with us). The man portion of Jesus would have human blood and the God portion of Jesus would not give in to the temptations that we all face. Jesus was tempted as we are and did not sin. He knows how we feel when tempted because he felt the same way.

Heb 4:15 For we have not an high priest which cannot be touched with the feeling of our infirmities; but was in all points tempted like as [we are, yet] without sin.

In order for Jesus to take away the sins of the world, they needed to be placed upon him. How could this happen? Jesus committed no sin! Somehow, God placed the sins of all mankind (past, present, and future) on Jesus Christ and then allowed Him to receive the punishment.

There is some debate as to when the sins of the world were placed on Jesus. I believe that it took place on His way to the garden of Gethsemane. The following scripture reveals that Jesus confesses that he is close to death for the first time in His life:

Matt 26: 36 ¶ Then cometh Jesus with them unto a place called Gethsemane, and saith unto the disciples, Sit ye here, while I go and pray yonder. **37** And he took with him Peter and the two sons of Zebedee, and began to be sorrowful and very heavy. **38** Then saith he unto them, *My soul is exceeding sorrowful, even unto death*: tarry ye here, and watch with me. **39** And he went a little further, and fell on his face, and prayed, saying, O my Father, if it be possible, let this cup pass from me: nevertheless not as I will, but as thou wilt. **40** And he cometh unto the disciples, and findeth them asleep, and saith unto Peter, What, could ye not watch with me one hour? **41** Watch and pray, that ye enter not into temptation: the spirit indeed is willing, but the flesh is weak. **42** He went away again the second time, and prayed, saying, O my Father, if this cup may not pass away from me, except I drink it, thy will be done. **43** And he came and found them asleep again: for their eyes were heavy. **44** And he left them, and went away again, and prayed the third time, saying the same words. **45** Then cometh he to his disciples, and saith unto them, Sleep on now, and take your rest: behold, the hour is at hand, and the Son of man is betrayed into the hands of sinners. **46** Rise, let us be going: behold, he is at hand that doth betray me.

It stands to reason that if the sins (death) of the world, past, present and future were placed on one man, His body would begin to buckle under the weight. It is with this reasoning that I believe that Jesus was asking God to let the cup of death of that moment pass from him so that he could make it to the cross. The punishment for the sins had not yet taken place and if he died at Gethsemane, mankind would still be lost without a way to reconcile completely with God. Jesus, being completely submitted to the Father, was willing to die there in the garden knowing that God would provide a more perfect way to reconcile mankind. However, Jesus was the perfect way and God sent angels to strengthen Him to make it to His final destination.

Luke 22:42 Saying, Father, if thou be willing, remove this cup from me: nevertheless not my will, but thine, be done. **43** And there appeared an angel unto him from heaven, strengthening him.

What a wonderful picture of submission! Everything was on the line, yet Jesus trusted the Father. How much more should we practice trusting Jesus even if everything is on the line?

Wait! It's not over! The judgment of sin still needed to be carried out. The bible records the things Jesus suffered for you and me:

1. He was betrayed by one of His closest members
2. He was apprehended like a thief in the night
3. He was brought before the Sanhedrin (the spiritual leaders) to be judged
4. The High Priest and Elders sought to put Him to death
5. They spit in His face
6. He was buffeted (Struck with the fist) by several
7. He was slapped by several

8. They taunted him as they smote Him while he was blind folded saying "Prophesy unto us, thou Christ, Who is he that smote thee?"
9. He was brought before a Roman leader (Pilate); like an outlaw.
10. He was falsely accused again.
11. A thief was chosen by the people to be released over Him (denied by His own people).
12. The people cried out "Crucify Jesus" to Pilate when he asked what he shall do to Jesus.
13. When Pilate washed his hands of the matter (he knew that Jesus was innocent) the people cried "His blood be on us and our children". He was despised!
14. He was scourged (beat with a whip that was knotted with metal pieces that tore his flesh) until he was near death.
15. A whole band of soldiers took Him and stripped Him and put on His bleeding back a scarlet robe.
16. A platted crown of thorns was pressed on His head which pierce His skull.
17. A reed placed in His hand and the soldiers bowed the knee before Him and mocked him, Him saying Hail King of the Jews!
18. He was spat upon by the soldiers.
19. The reed was taken and used to hit him on the head.
20. The scarlet robe was pulled off His back to start the bleeding again. They ignored his critical condition.
21. He was lead to be crucified (He was unable to carry the cross, Simon of Cyrene bore his cross).
22. He was offered vinegar mixed with something bitter to drink at the place he was to be crucified.
23. He was nailed through His feet and hands to the cross.

24. He suffered extreme pain and suffocation with his weight on the nails through His hands.
25. He suffered extreme pain and His knees buckled when he pushed up on the nail through His feet to gasp for air.
26. His clothes were cut in pieces and His vesture (cloak) was gambled away by the soldiers.
27. Many mocked Him on the cross saying "If thou be the Son of God, come down from the cross." The chief priests with the scribes mocked "He saved others; himself he cannot save. If he be the King of Israel, let him now come down from the cross, and we will believe him. He trusted in God; let him deliver him now, if he will have him: for he said, I am the Son of God."
28. The two thieves who were crucified with Him also mocked Him.
29. To properly punish the sin, God forsook (turned His back on) Jesus.
30. JESUS DIED!
31. Already dead, He was pierced in His side by a spear from a Roman Soldier.

This should give you a good idea of the punishment that is designated for sin. I am sure that you can relate to some of these sufferings personally.

LOVE IS NOT A FEELING! IT IS A COMMITMENT!

If love is a feeling, then Jesus would not have committed to suffer all these things so that we could have a relationship with God.

WAIT! THERE IS GOOD NEWS!

Jesus rose from the grave on the third day!

1Corinthians (1Cor) 15:1 ¶ Moreover, brethren, I declare unto you the gospel which I preached unto you, which also ye have received, and wherein ye stand; **2** By which also ye are saved, if ye keep in memory what I preached unto you, unless ye have believed in vain. **3** For I delivered unto you first of all that which I also received, how that ***Christ died for our sins according to the scriptures; 4 And that he was buried, and that he rose again the third day*** according to the scriptures: **5** And that he was seen of Cephas, then of the twelve: **6** After that, he was seen of above five hundred brethren at once; of whom the greater part remain unto this present, but some are fallen asleep. **7** After that, he was seen of James; then of all the apostles. **8** And last of all he was seen of me also, as of one born out of due time.

Jesus is alive! Death could only kill the sin, not the sinless blood! Jesus' humanity was destroyed because the sins of the world were upon it. His deity could not be held by the grave. Jesus is able to give us life because He lives today! This is why Jesus said:

John 10:10 The thief cometh not, but for to steal, and to kill, and to destroy: ***I am come that they might have life, and that they might have [it] more abundantly.***

I hope that you see the following scripture differently now:

Joh 3:16 For God so loved the world, that he gave his only begotten Son, that whosoever believeth in him should not perish, but have everlasting life. **17** For God sent not his Son into the world to condemn the world; but that the world through him might be saved. **18** He that believeth on him is not condemned: but he that believeth not is condemned already, because he hath not believed in the name of the only begotten Son of God.

1.3

Salvation Summary

Below is a basic summary of things we received when we ask Jesus to come into our heart:

1. We are saved from the law of sin and death
2. All of our sins past, present, and future are forgiven
3. We become part of the family of God
4. Our relationship with God has begun
5. God hears our prayers
6. We received Grace; unmerited favor of God
7. We receive Mercy; not receiving what we deserve
8. We receive forgiveness and are required to forgive
9. We are obligated to learn more of Jesus through the bible, church and prayer
10. We receive the ministry of reconciliation; we have the obligation and right to witness to others
11. All of our needs are met according to the riches of God (Philippians 4: 19)
12. And many more blessings that are not covered here

Ps 68:19 Blessed [be] the Lord, [who] **daily** loadeth us [with benefits, even] the God of our salvation. Selah.

I think it's time to start using our daily load of benefits! Don't you? Besides, you get a whole new load tomorrow.

1.4

Receiving Forgiveness & Forgiving

Once we have received Jesus Christ as our Lord and Savior, we are immediately forgiven of our past sins. When Jesus died and rose again, he gave provision for forgiveness for all past present and future sins; this is the only way he could affect the future generations. So it is no surprise when I tell you that Jesus has already forgiven all your past, present and future sins. This is not to say that we can behave without restraint. John wrote to the Christians to confess their sins.

1Joh 1:9 If we confess our sins, he is faithful and just to forgive us [our] sins, and to cleanse us from all unrighteousness.

The Greek meaning for "confess our sins" implies that we speak out loud our departure from the way that we have committed to follow. All we are required to do is confess our sins to Him and He will forgive us and cleanse us! Hallelujah! Jesus' level of forgiveness is complete. He said:

Matt 12:31 Wherefore I say unto you, **All manner of sin and blasphemy shall be forgiven unto men:** but the blasphemy [against] the [Holy] Ghost shall not be forgiven unto men. **32** And whosoever speaketh a word against the Son of man, it shall be forgiven him: but whosoever speaketh against the Holy Ghost, it shall not be forgiven him, neither in this world, neither in the [world] to come.

There is no sin that you can commit that God will not forgive but the blasphemy of the Holy Ghost. Even if you speak against the Father, Jesus or Christianity, God will forgive you if you ask Him to. When God forgives your sin, your relationship with Him is restored and you have free access to your Father in heaven.

Now some of you may be wondering if you have committed blasphemy or spoke against the Holy Ghost. Let's look at some Greek Definitions to clarify this:

> Blasphemy in the Greek is βλασφημια blasphemia (pronounced blas-fay-me'-ah)
>
> > 1) slander, detraction, speech injurious, to another's good name
> > 2) impious and reproachful speech injurious to divine majesty
>
> And Holy Ghost in the Greek is πνευμα pneuma (pronounced pnyoo'-mah) meaning:
>
> > 1) the third person of the triune God, the Holy Spirit, coequal, coeternal with the Father and the Son
> > > 1a) sometimes referred to in a way which emphasizes his personality and character (the Holy Spirit)
> > > 1b) sometimes referred to in a way which emphasizes his work and power (the Spirit of Truth)
> > > 1c) never referred to as a depersonalized force

If you are still concerned whether you have committed this unpardonable sin, let me remind you that a person who is guilty of this sin would not be reading this book for a closer walk with Jesus. Also, Apostle Paul persecuted Christians to death before he became one of the most dynamic preachers for Christ (he was forgiven).

THE EXTENT OF GOD'S FORGIVENESS

To what extent does God go to when He forgives? Let's see what the scriptures say.

Ps 103:12 As far as the east is from the west, [so] far hath he removed our transgressions from us.

When my children were very young, from time to time they would get dirty from playing with their food or at the play ground. My wife or I would need to clean them up. We washed them with soap and water and would drain the water to remove the dirt far away from them. This is how God forgives us; he separates us from our sins completely.

Additionally, some have said that when they forgive, they don't forget. I wonder if they really forgave. You see, God does not treat us that way; He forgets about our sins.

Heb 10:15 [Whereof] the Holy Ghost also is a witness to us: for after that he had said before, 16 This [is] the covenant that I will make with them after those days, saith the Lord, I will put my laws into their hearts, and in their minds will I write them;   17 **And their sins and iniquities will I remember no more.**

It would stand to reason that if our Heavenly Father forgives and forgets, then we should also do the same.

WHAT IS OUR ROLE IN FORGIVENESS?

If I receive forgiveness from the Father, then I have to let it go myself. Imagine asking the Father to forgive you for something and He separates it from you and forgets about it. Then you go to Him again repenting about the very same sin because you have not let it go. The Father might look at Jesus, shrug His shoulders and say "What is he/she talking about?" Jesus looks at the Holy Ghost and does the same. Finally, the Holy Ghost is stuck with the question that He cannot answer and he has no one to pass it on to. Don't do that to the heavenly host! All kidding aside, I encourage you to accept the grace, mercy and forgiveness you have received.

One of Jesus' greatest lessons was His sermon on the mountain. Matthew chapters 5, 6, and 7 capture this event. In the middle of his lesson, he taught us how to pray. This prayer contains a book of material in the prayer itself but I want to focus on His directive to forgive.

Matt 6:9 ¶ After this manner therefore pray ye: Our Father which art in heaven, Hallowed be thy name. **10** Thy kingdom come. Thy will be done in earth, as it is in heaven. **11** Give us this day our daily bread. **12 And forgive us our debts, as we forgive our debtors. 13** And lead us not into temptation, but deliver us from evil: For thine is the kingdom, and the power, and the glory, forever. Amen. **14 For if ye forgive men their trespasses, your heavenly Father will also forgive you: 15 But if ye forgive not men their trespasses, neither will your Father forgive your trespasses.**

Jesus makes it an imperative that we maintain forgiveness with God when we forgive others. To do that, we must forgive others. Forgiving others is better done when we understand the forgiveness, mercy, and grace that we have received from the father; this is why I placed this important lesson behind the Mercy and Grace sections. It should be out of our gratitude of the forgiveness that we have received that gives us strength to forgive others. Here is an example of this principle.

Mt 18:21 ¶ Then came Peter to him, and said, Lord, how oft shall my brother sin against me, and I forgive him? till seven times? **22** Jesus saith unto him, I say not unto thee, Until seven times: but, Until seventy times seven. **23** Therefore is the kingdom of heaven likened unto a certain king, which would take account of his servants. **24** And when he had begun to reckon, one was brought unto him, which owed him ten thousand talents. **25** But forasmuch as he had not to pay, his lord commanded him to be sold, and his wife, and children, and all that he had, and payment to be made. **26** The servant therefore fell down, and worshipped him, saying, Lord, have patience with me, and I will pay thee all. **27** Then the lord of that servant was moved with compassion, and loosed him, and forgave him the debt. **28** But the same servant went out, and found one of his fellowservants, which owed him an hundred pence: and he laid hands on him, and took [him] by the throat, saying, Pay me that thou owest. **29** And his fellowservant fell down at his feet, and besought him, saying, Have patience with me, and I will pay thee all. **30** And he would not: but went and cast him into prison, till he should pay the debt. **31** So when his fellowservants saw what was done, they were very sorry, and came and told unto their lord all that was done. **32** Then his lord, after that he had called him, said unto him, O thou wicked servant, I forgave thee all that debt, because thou desiredst me: **33** Shouldest not thou also have had compassion on thy fellowservant, even as I had pity on thee? **34** And his lord was wroth, and delivered him to the tormentors, till he should pay all that was due unto him. **35** So likewise shall my heavenly Father do also unto you, if ye from your hearts forgive not everyone his brother their trespasses.

This is why forgiving is so important to us. The Father desires for us to forgive as we are forgiven. When God forgives us, he forgets about it.

We must remember that forgiveness is not a feeling; it is an act of our will. If we are offended, then our feelings will want to hold the offense against someone. We as Christians forgive by decision because it is the will of the Father and we forgive as He does…we forget about it.

MY TESTAMONY

When I first received Jesus into my heart, I was struggling with getting high. My guilt and condemnation was so much that every sermon I heard seemed to speak against it. I prayed and sought Jesus to help me quit for weeks when He finally led me to my need to forgive my father. I wanted nothing to do with this subject but I could no longer resist it. It took me about three months to get my head and heart right to call my father. I told him that I forgave him for the things that he did to me. He replied "I don't know what you are talking about." The next Sunday after church I sat in the same car, in the same seat with the same person that I got high with and when he offered it to me, I thought I was going to throw up! I couldn't do it! Since that time, I have never had a need or a desire to get high again. Praise the Lord!

The lesson that I learned here is that our actions are an effect of our heart. The cause is what is in our heart. If I fix the cause, the effect will go away. My unforgiveness of my father was keeping me bound to other sins. Once I forgave my father, regardless of his response, I was set free from an entanglement that I could shake on my own.

Forgiveness is a powerful weapon against the snares of the enemy. Do not underestimate how the enemy will try to encourage you to keep an issue with someone. You will hear all sorts of justifications to hold a grudge in your thoughts and from others. But God could have done the same to us; instead He died on the Cross. It didn't feel good but it was necessary. Forgiving may be difficult, but it is necessary.

It is my experience that forgiving others is not for them but for me. Doctors have confirmed that biologically, it is unhealthy to harbor ill will against someone. When I forgive someone, I release the pressures off of my life. I am willing to believe that Jesus had us in mind when he stressed the need to forgive.

I am reminded of a woman who the Holy Spirit revealed to me that she was harboring unforgiveness against a man who physically abused her. As I prayed for her, the Lord led me to insist that she speak out that she forgives him. She struggled and strained to frame the words and finally she said them. It was clear that these were the hardest words that she had ever tried to speak. Once she succeeded, a spirit of relief came over her and she wept in ecstasy as the Holy Ghost began to pour into her and minister to her needs. She was truly set free that day!

God is very interested in our ability to get along with others. To the point that Jesus gave these instructions:

Matt 5:23 Therefore if thou bring thy gift to the altar, and there rememberest that thy brother hath ought against thee; **24** Leave there thy gift before the altar, and go thy way; first be reconciled to thy brother, and then come and offer thy gift.

Let's be diligent at keeping unforgiveness out of our heart!

When we forgive, we win and the testimony of Christ wins! Let's stay in the WIN – WIN business!

You must then bless the one you are forgiving. Jesus said:

Mt 5:44 But I say unto you, Love your enemies, bless them that curse you, do good to them that hate you, and pray for them which despitefully use you, and persecute you;

Your success from getting free of the bondage of unforgiveness is hinged on whether you learn to forgive AND bless those who have offended you.

HOW DO I FORGIVE?

1. Choose to forgive
2. Speak out your forgiveness aloud often
3. Bless the one you are forgiving in prayer

Here is an example prayer:

Lord Jesus, forgive me of all my sins, known and unknown according to your word. Help me to stay in forgiveness as you forgive me. I forgive (name). Now I bless (name) and pray that you touch them and move on their behalf for your cause.

1.5

There Are Some Obligations You Have Towards God

There are some who believe that once we get saved, we are finished. However, getting saved is about starting a relationship with Jesus Christ. As in all balanced relationships, there is a commitment to the relationship from both parties. If we are to take full advantage of the benefits of salvation, then we must continue to follow our Lord's direction. Jesus **will not fail** in His obligations to us. So let's look at one instruction concerning our relationship with our Lord. We will cover this scripture more closely in another section of this book. For now, just know that Jesus is letting us know what to do and the results for doing them.

Matt 11:28 Come unto me, all [ye] that labour and are heavy laden, and I will give you rest. **29** Take my yoke upon you, and learn of me; for I am meek and lowly in heart: and ye shall find rest unto your souls. **30** For my yoke [is] easy, and my burden is light.

So here are some obligations you now have. These are vital to your success in your development.

1. Pray (talk with Jesus) daily.

2. Find a church that will teach you more of Jesus from the Bible.

3. Read the Bible daily.

   3a. Start with John in the New Testament and read twice.

3b.   Then begin with Matthew and read the New Testament Three times.

3c.   Then begin with Genesis and read the whole Bible. Repeat once finished.

4. Seek more of Jesus Christ to include receiving the baptism of the Holy Ghost and to be baptized in water according to the scriptures.

Remember that God's principles operate on His word alone. Just like gravity, no matter whom you are or how you feel, if you work with it, it will help you, if you work against it, it will hurt you!

1.6

The Principles of Life & Death

In the beginning God not only created the heavens and the earth, he also established the principles that would frame all that was created. Gravity, inertia, centrifugal force and many others were put in place to support the balance of the heavens and the earth.

A principle is an undisputable law that will consistently respond within specific parameters. It will help us if we work within its parameters or it will defy us if we choose to work against it.

There are two such principles that I would like to mention here: The *Law of sin and Death* and *Life is in the Blood*. These two principles are opposites. Clearly, Life is the opposite of death and by association; blood is the opposite of sin.

Our current initial state as humans is in death as we are the children of fallen Adam and Eve. For this reason, I will begin with where we are and take us to where God wants us; LIFE!

1. The Law of Sin and Death

God in his infinite wisdom set the principle of sin and death in place and told Adam about it in Genesis 2:17. Incidentally, disobedience to God is sin, which brings death.

Genesis (Gen) 2:17 But of the tree of the knowledge of good and evil, thou shalt not eat of it: for in the day that thou eatest thereof thou shalt surely die.

Every time sin is present (disobedience to God), death is right there beside it. This principle is true to all, whether you are a Christian or a non believer. It is like the principle of gravity; it is undisputedly consistent.

2. Life is in the Blood

Leviticus (Lev) 17:11 For the life of the flesh [is] in the blood: and I have given it to you upon the altar to make an atonement for your souls: for it [is] the blood [that] maketh an atonement for the soul.

God also set this principle to counter death. We all know that the opposite of death is life, here the scriptures point out that the opposite of sin is blood.

Rom 8:2 For the law of the Spirit of life in Christ Jesus hath made me free from the law of sin and death.

Before the sin of Adam and Eve, God was able to enjoy the relationship with Adam and Eve freely. Nothing prevented or stood between God and Man because Man was naked and without sin before a holy God. God is so holy that if anything unrighteous, defiled or sinful approaches Him, it is destroyed. Now God was faced with dealing with the sin of Adam and Eve in the Garden of Eden. Adam and Eve could not approach God with the sin of disobedience upon them. So God shed blood to oppose the sin and death on Adam and Eve to keep the relationship going. God has always made provisions to preserve a pathway for man to commune with Him.

Gen 3:21 ¶ Unto Adam also and to his wife did the LORD God make coats of skins, and clothed them.

I think we all can agree that in order to make coats of skins, blood was shed. So from the very beginning, blood was used to allow man to continue his relationship with God.
The love that God has for us is so great that he shed blood to keep the relationship with man and Himself alive. No man can approach God with death (sin) on them. Jesus told the Sadducees that God was a God of the living not the dead. You see death and life are just like day and night; Life will drive the death away when it is present.

Matt 22:32 I am the God of Abraham, and the God of Isaac, and the God of Jacob? God is not the God of the dead, but of the living.

So when we sin, we bring a portion of death upon us. When we ask Jesus to forgive us, we are applying Jesus' blood to our lives so that we can maintain our walk with Jesus and live. 1 John 1:9 was written for the Christian, not the unbeliever.

1 John (1Joh) 1:9 If we confess our sins, he is faithful and just to forgive us [our] sins, and to cleanse us from all unrighteousness.

It's common for a Christian to spend time confessing their sins to Jesus in prayer. Confessing is like taking a shower; you are cleansed by the blood and can walk on with Jesus. So remember that confession is cleansing. Sometimes you clean up more often than others. It's OK! We all go through times of constant repentance, less times of repentance and then back to constant repentance. This cycle is the life of a true Christian; this is considered normal.

If someone has told you that once you ask Jesus into your heart, you are finished, they are mistaken. In order for you to give your life to Jesus, it will take you a lifetime. Your spirit man is saved completely. It is your body and soul that will require development. Development comes from practicing to apply the word of God. When you fall short: pick yourself up, ask Jesus to forgive you, and press on with your development. Remember, the art of learning is repetition.

1Joh 1:9 If we confess our sins, he is faithful and just to forgive us [our] sins, and to cleanse us from all unrighteousness.

1.7

Separate Yourself

When God began Abram's transformation into the father of many nations, He started it by one directive; Separate yourself.

Gen 12:1 ¶ Now the LORD had said unto Abram, Get thee out of thy country, and from thy kindred, and from thy father's house, unto a land that I will shew thee: **2** And I will make of thee a great nation, and I will bless thee, and make thy name great; and thou shalt be a blessing: **3** And I will bless them that bless thee, and curse him that curseth thee: and in thee shall all families of the earth be blessed. **4** ¶ So Abram departed, as the LORD had spoken unto him; and Lot went with him: and Abram [was] seventy and five years old when he departed out of Haran.

If you were to look up the Hebrew meaning of Haran, you would find: חָרָן Charan (pronounced kaw-rawn') meaning mountaineer. This is intriguing because all mountaineers are sure footed for obvious reasons. Abram's lifestyle was centered on careful planning to ensure safe passage through the mountains. Yet, despite his nature of being sure footed, he obeyed God and left the security of what he was familiar with. For the relationship with God, he forsook his relatives, friends, home, community, and his own nature. Abram must have had a powerful experience with God to contradict his nature and training to venture out with only a promise. I wonder how many comments were made to him by his family and friends as he prepared and made his departure. This is not unlike today. As you seek to know Jesus, many will have some hurtful things to say because they have not experienced what you have. The difficulty is trying to get someone who does not believe to understand what you are doing; it cannot be done. However, with God, loss always brings great gain!

The principle of separating yourself from your comfortable surroundings is inevitable if you intend to continue with the Lord Jesus. As you can see from Genises 12:1 - 4, it is not to hurt you; rather to bring you to your predestined destination. You are a work of the Lord and He has a special purpose for you. Just like Abram, if you will follow Jesus, all your dreams will come true. Remember, Jesus is the dream giver and the dream fulfiller!

I am not saying that you should leave your home, family, friends, job etc… I am saying be aware that Jesus is going to separate you from some things to make your relationship with Him the highest priority. He does not desire for you to be around those who influence you to do or say things that are not pleasing to Him. If you find yourself among those types of people, kindly excuse yourself.

One thing that helped me greatly was going to the house of God. I went every time the doors were opened. This is a good way to change your habits. And let's face it; it is a great way to hide from those you are not ready to face just now.

Additionally, working in the house of the Lord has some helpful benefits.

Proverbs (Prov) 16:3 ¶ Commit thy works unto the LORD, and thy thoughts shall be established.

New or Old, Christians get a better handle on their thought life when they begin to participate in meeting the needs of the church. You don't have to be perfect, talented, or knowledgeable to join an auxiliary and become active in the church. You just need to be willing. A willing heart can change the world.

MY TESTAMONY

When I first got saved, Sunday, May 2, 1982, I wanted to do everything the Lord would allow me to do for Him. I feel that way today. So I did some yard work, cleaned the church bathrooms, lifted heavy things... I came around and did whatever they asked. I was dealing with a lot of issues and working at the church gave so much relief from them that I spent a huge amount of time there. As time went on and my military travels moved me, I would volunteer for whatever needed to be done where I went to church. Over the years I became a cleaner, a sound man, counselor and many other positions. Just let God use you as He sees fit. At first, just meet the church needs with whatever you are able to provide; your time, money, gifts and talents. Let it grow from there.

God never takes anything away without replacing it. Remember, it is easier to pour more water into an unfilled glass than a full one. God empties you out from time to time to give you more of what you did not know that you needed. Soon you will trust Him completely and know that He is looking out for your best interests.

Rom 8:28 And we know that all things work together for good to them that love God, to them who are the called according to [his] purpose.

I ministered in Charleston, S.C. to a musician who truly had the gift of music from God. He also was struggling with homosexuality. God told me to tell him that if he would separate himself from his old crowd, that He would turn his life around dramatically. Seven years later I learned that he received the word I gave him and obeyed. The Lord kept His word and now he is married with children and going strong for the Lord. Praise the Lord. Separating yourself to the Lord is a powerful action!

Ezra 10:11 Now therefore make confession unto the LORD God of your fathers, and do his pleasure: and separate yourselves from the people of the land, and from the strange wives.

Separating ourselves helps us be who God has made us to be:

1Peter (1Pet) 2:9 But ye [are] a chosen generation, a royal priesthood, an holy nation, a peculiar people; that ye should shew forth the praises of him who hath called you out of darkness into his marvellous light: **10** Which in time past [were] not a people, but [are] now the people of God: which had not obtained mercy, but now have obtained mercy.   **11** Dearly beloved, I beseech [you] as strangers and pilgrims, abstain from fleshly lusts, which war against the soul;   **12** Having your conversation honest among the Gentiles: that, whereas they speak against you as evildoers, they may by [your] good works, which they shall behold, glorify God in the day of visitation.

1.8

Grace: Unmerited Favor

Ephesians (Eph) 2:8 For by grace are ye saved through faith; and that not of yourselves: [it is] the gift of God: **9** Not of works, lest any man should boast.

If we were to make a dish called salvation, we would need two main ingredients: grace and faith. God gives us grace and by it we are saved through our faith. It is by grace and through faith. The grace that we receive comes from God and is fully mature. Immediately we are given the full measure of grace upon salvation; God can give no more and he will not give any less. Our faith comes by believing that Jesus Christ died on the cross for our sins and rose again on the third day. It is that faith that salvation comes through.

We cannot save ourselves; we do not have the ability or the resources to do so. It is truly by the gift of God that we can be saved at all. We can't earn it, we can't do anything for it, we can't buy it and we can't negotiate for it. All we have to do is believe that Jesus Christ is the son of God and that he died on the cross for our sins and rose again on the third day. That sparks enough faith for salvation to come through.

Eph 2:9 says "not of works". Our society teaches us that in order for us to be good we have to do good things. We have to earn our way through; no pain no gain. This is not the case with salvation and the things of God, God wanted to make sure that all could be saved regardless of their capabilities, talents and works so he provided it as a gift. Now all we have to do is receive it.

Merriam-Webster defines grace as **1 a:** unmerited divine assistance given humans for their regeneration or sanctification **b:** a virtue coming from God **c:** a state of sanctification enjoyed through divine grace. **2 a:** Approval, favor <stayed in his good *graces*> **b:** *archaic*: mercy, pardon **c:** a special favor

In my discussion with other Christians I have heard them say "unmerited favor". In other words, we have grace, favor, approval, and pardon that we didn't earn. Isn't that wonderful news? Grace allows us to prosper when we stand in a barren land. As we seek Jesus, He will give us direction to do the right thing at the right time to succeed when all others are failing.

In the balance of things, God gives us grace but He does not want us to continue in sin.

Rom 6:1 ¶ What shall we say then? Shall we continue in sin, that grace may abound? **2** God forbid. How shall we, that are dead to sin, live any longer therein?

Rom 6:12 Let not sin therefore reign in your mortal body, that ye should obey it in the lusts thereof. **13** Neither yield ye your members [as] instruments of unrighteousness unto sin: but yield yourselves unto God, as those that are alive from the dead, and your members [as] instruments of righteousness unto God. **14** For sin shall not have dominion over you: **for ye are not under the law, but under grace**. **15** What then? shall we sin, because we are not under the law, but under grace? God forbid.

Grace has a mindset that, at first glance, appears to disregard the law of God. Let's look at these two principles to better understand the balance. If we understand the mindset of the Law and the mindset of Grace, we will be able to walk with Jesus more perfectly.

THE LAW

In order to have the correct perspective of the law, let's look at its purpose. If we know the purpose of a thing, we will not abuse it and it will not abuse us.

THE PURPOSE OF THE LAW

In order for us to identify something wrong, we must be told what is wrong. If we are told that everything is good, then how will we be able to determine if something is wrong? For this reason the Law was given to identify what is wrong.

Rom 7:7 ¶ What shall we say then? [Is] the law sin? God forbid. Nay, I had not known sin, but by the law: for I had not known lust, except the law had said, Thou shalt not covet.

When a parent is teaching a child, the first thing they do is identify things that they should and shouldn't do. This is vital for the child's safety because the child cannot comprehend the full consequences of touching a hot burner on the stove. It is out of love and concern that the parent does this; to protect the child from needless harm.

For this reason, the Father gave us the Law to identify what is hazardous to our lives so that we don't suffer unknown consequences needlessly.

THE CONCLUSION OF THE LAW

Now that we know that the Law identifies what to do and not to do, sin is identified when we are contrary to the law. We can conclude that when we disobey the law, we sin.

1John (1Joh) 3:4 ¶ Whosoever committeth sin transgresseth also the law: for sin is the transgression of the law.

Anyone who desires to avoid sin will see that it is impossible to live sinless.

James (Jas) 2:10 For whosoever shall keep the whole law, and yet offend in one [point], he is guilty of all.

It is impossible for a human to keep the whole law! Finally, we must come to a conclusion that we need a savior to help us out of this impossible predicament. **This is the point that the Law was designed to bring us.** We cannot succeed without help. That help has come through our Lord Jesus Christ by Grace! Hallelujah!

THE MINDSET OF THE LAW

1Cor 15:56 The sting of death [is] sin; and the strength of sin [is] the law.

We now know that sin has no strength without the law. If sin had no strength, then we could resist all sin and be perfect here on this earth.

But legalists will tell you that the law must be obeyed! Hence, pointing out our sins and inability to avoid sin and cause us to be discouraged that we have fallen to sin. This is not Life! Nor is it the purpose of the law.

Rom 8:2 For the law of the Spirit of life in Christ Jesus hath made me free from the law of sin and death.

You are under attack of the Law Mentality when:
- you are reminded that you have failed.
- you are told or think that you are going to suffer because you did something wrong.
- you are reminded of your past failures out of accusation (not for a lesson learned).

- you think you have failed because you did or did not do something.
- you think you have fallen short to deserve anything and have given up.

Run to Jesus and His Grace!

THE MINDSET OF GRACE

Let me speak with you here on a personal level. Not all your thoughts are yours. The enemy is legalistic and he will fire many darts at your thoughts that remind you of your short comings. He may say "You did not pray today so don't expect God to protect you!" If you agree with this thought then you give strength to sin and step outside the protection of Grace. You must reject these thoughts immediately by using the word of God. Whenever you are under attack and you are bombarded with accusations of your faults, failures, and inadequacies quote:

Rom 8:2 For the law of the Spirit of life in Christ Jesus hath made me free from the law of sin and death.

On a side note, do you really think that the Grace of God is dependent on what you do or don't do? That is a law mentality that limits what Jesus did for you.

You see, Jesus died for all past, present and future sins 2000 years ago. Your past sins were considered future sins when Jesus died for them. So it is reasonable to say that He has died for your future sins as well. Grace!

Don't step out of the covering of Grace and allow yourself to think negative thoughts about yourself. When you do, you give sin strength. You have been set free to walk in faith with Jesus Christ because He loves you unconditionally.

By now if you are a "by the book person", you are about to put this book down. **Don't stop reading!** There is a balance to all things including Grace! You see, we should not be striving to be like Jesus using the law. We should be striving to be like Him by Grace! Here is why:

Did you know that the last verse in the bible bestows Grace upon us? Yes, here it is:

Revelations (Rev) 22:21 The grace of our Lord Jesus Christ [be] with you all. Amen.

Grace is defined in the Greek as χαρις charis (pronounced khar'-ece); which has several meanings but I will share just a few here.

1. that which affords joy, pleasure, delight, sweetness, charm, loveliness: grace of speech
2. good will, loving-kindness, favor
3. of the merciful kindness by which God, exerting his holy influence upon souls, turns them to Christ, keeps, strengthens, increases them in Christian faith, knowledge, affection, and kindles them to the exercise of the Christian virtues
4. **the spiritual condition of one governed by the power of divine grace**

Take note of number 4. If we allow grace to govern us:
- it will provoke us to have a controlled speech.
- we will seek good will and loving-kindness.
- we will continue to turn to Christ for strength and faith.
- it will increase our knowledge about Him.
- it will cause us to exercise Christian virtues.
- we will be governed by the power of divine grace.

Although grace is unmerited favor, it is also an influence to do the right thing. We are no longer under the Old

Testament of law because Jesus died and left a last will and testament of grace that we should be governed by. Here I'd like to point out that it is good to study the Old Testament to learn more about Jesus after you have a good understanding of Jesus in the New Testament.

So when someone continues in sin and says "God knows my heart" or "I am under Grace", ask them if they truly understand the purpose of God's divine grace and its governing power. Many times we are ignorant of the depths of the Grace of God.

LAW & GRACE MENTALITY

Here are some scenarios that may help you better understand the difference between a Law Mentality and Grace Mentality:

1. Scenario 1

   a. Law mentality – You didn't read your bible today, or do what your church says you should do. So you feel bad and feel like you missed a blessing and will pay for it later – you are giving strength to sin and frustrating Grace.
   b. Grace mentality – You didn't read your bible today, or do what your church says you should do so you press on because you realize that only Jesus is perfect and expect Him to do something great for you today – you are pleasing the Lord.

2. Scenario 2

   a. Law mentality – You committed a sin and asked Jesus to forgive you. Yet you continue to anguish over it and tear yourself down – you are giving strength to sin and frustrating Grace.

b. Grace mentality – You committed a sin and asked Jesus to forgive you. Now you are pressing on to do better with the mindset that you are forgetting the torment of the past and getting back up to walk with Jesus because you know that you are forgiven – you are pleasing the Lord.

To choose a "Grace Mentality" you will have to discipline your thinking to reject the legalistic mentality (you will get what you deserve and you no longer have favor with God). Yes, there are consequences for our decisions and actions, some greater than others, but it does not separate you from the Grace and Love of God!

Rom 8:34 Who is he that condemneth? It is Christ that died, yea rather, that is risen again, who is even at the right hand of God, who also maketh intercession for us. **35** Who shall separate us from the love of Christ? shall tribulation, or distress, or persecution, or famine, or nakedness, or peril, or sword? **36** As it is written, For thy sake we are killed all the day long; we are accounted as sheep for the slaughter. **37** Nay, in all these things we are more than conquerors through him that loved us. **38** For I am persuaded, that neither death, nor life, nor angels, nor principalities, nor powers, nor things present, nor things to come, **39** Nor height, nor depth, nor any other creature, shall be able to separate us from the love of God, which is in Christ Jesus our Lord.

God wants us to be so Grace minded that the last verse in the bible is:

Rev 22:21 The **grace** of our Lord Jesus Christ [be] with you all. Amen.

In summary, the law was established to point out a need for a deliverer. A new order of faith in Jesus Christ was established to provide the deliverance we need from sin.

Galatians (Gal) 3:23 But before faith came, we were kept under the law, shut up unto the faith which should afterwards be revealed. **24** Wherefore the law was our schoolmaster [to bring us] unto Christ, that we might be justified by faith. **25** But after that faith is come, we are no longer under a schoolmaster. **26** For ye are all the children of God by faith in Christ Jesus. **27** For as many of you as have been baptized into Christ have put on Christ. **28** There is neither Jew nor Greek, there is neither bond nor free, there is neither male nor female: for ye are all one in Christ Jesus. **29** And if ye [be] Christ's, then are ye Abraham's seed, and heirs according to the promise.

Gal 4:1 ¶ Now I say, [That] the heir, as long as he is a child, differeth nothing from a servant, though he be lord of all; **2** But is under tutors and governors until the time appointed of the father. **3** Even so we, when we were children, were in bondage under the elements of the world: **4** But when the fulness of the time was come, God sent forth his Son, made of a woman, made under the law, **5** To redeem them that were under the law, that we might receive the adoption of sons. **6** And because ye are sons, God hath sent forth the Spirit of his Son into your hearts, crying, Abba, Father. **7** Wherefore thou art no more a servant, but a son; and if a son, then an heir of God through Christ.

The new testament of the Lord Jesus Christ gives us Grace to walk in newness of life. We are now a son and heir of God through Christ.

1.9

Mercy: Getting Better Than You Deserve

Once we have asked Jesus Christ into our hearts, we receive the Mercy of God. The Merriam-Webster's 11th Collegiate Dictionary defines Mercy as:

- compassion or forbearance shown especially to an offender or to one subject to one's power.
- lenient or compassionate treatment.
- a blessing that is an act of divine favor or compassion: a fortunate circumstance.

I see Mercy as getting better treatment than I deserve. You see, we were born in sin and shaped in iniquity from the womb because of the sinful nature passed on to us from Adam. Sin brings death and death is what we deserve. But God, in His infinite wisdom, sent his son Jesus Christ, to bare this punishment for us so that we could receive salvation (LIFE). That is true Mercy! Praise the Lord! Mercy exchanges the deserved punishment with the undeserved kindness. Let's look at how God has been exchanging what we deserve with what we don't throughout the bible. In Isaiah 61:3:

Isaiah (Isa) 61:3 To appoint unto them that mourn in Zion, to give unto them beauty for ashes, the oil of joy for mourning, the garment of praise for the spirit of heaviness; that they might be called trees of righteousness, the planting of the LORD, that he might be glorified.

God has been exchanging our negatives with His positives since Adam and Eve. Jesus, following in God the Father's footsteps, also said in John 10:10:

John 10:10 The thief cometh not, but for to steal, and to kill, and to destroy: I am come that they might have life, and that they might have [it] more abundantly. **11** I am the good shepherd: the good shepherd giveth his life for the sheep.

The Mercy we receive from Jesus Christ is not dependent on our ability to forgive ourselves. Although, we should forgive ourselves as Christ has forgiven us. It doesn't change the fact that we have Mercy at salvation. When a person has experienced Mercy, they become very grateful. I pray that we never lose our gratitude to the Lord. Here is a beautiful picture of love and gratitude because of Jesus' Mercy.

Luke 7:40 And Jesus answering said unto him, Simon, I have somewhat to say unto thee. And he saith, Master, say on. **41** There was a certain creditor which had two debtors: the one owed five hundred pence, and the other fifty. **42** And when they had nothing to pay, he frankly forgave them both. Tell me therefore, which of them will love him most? **43** Simon answered and said, I suppose that he, to whom he forgave most. And he said unto him, Thou hast rightly judged. **44** And he turned to the woman, and said unto Simon, Seest thou this woman? I entered into thine house, thou gavest me no water for my feet: but she hath washed my feet with tears, and wiped them with the hairs of her head. **45** Thou gavest me no kiss: but this woman since the time I came in hath not ceased to kiss my feet. **46** My head with oil thou didst not anoint: but this woman hath anointed my feet with ointment. **47** Wherefore I say unto thee, Her sins, which are many, are forgiven; for she loved much: but to whom little is forgiven, the same loveth little.

The woman at Jesus' feet received better than what she deserved and she knew it. Are we not like her? If Jesus came and sat down before us, wouldn't we be overwhelmed by His Mercy towards us and respond according to our gratitude for it? Even reading this passage I find myself no better than her and well up with humble gratitude for His Mercy towards me because I know I don't deserve it. His Mercy endures forever!

The Mercy that comes from the Lord Jesus Christ is one that pours out of His compassion towards us and He gives it freely to all who come to Him. God has given all of His Mercy; He will give no less and cannot give any more.

1Pe 1:3 ¶ Blessed [be] the God and Father of our Lord Jesus Christ, which according to his abundant mercy hath begotten us again unto a lively hope by the resurrection of Jesus Christ from the dead,

The Greek Definition for Mercy in this text is ελεος eleos pronounced (el'-eh-os) meaning:

- mercy: kindness or good will towards the miserable and the afflicted, joined with a desire to help them
- of God towards men: in general providence; the mercy and clemency of God in providing and offering to men salvation by Christ
- the mercy of Christ, whereby at his return to judgment he will bless true Christians with eternal life

It's clear here that God not only wants to extend kindness and goodwill towards you, He wants to help you through life as well.

1.10

The Ministry of Reconciliation

Once we have received Jesus Christ as our Lord and Savior, we are immediately given the ministry of reconciliation. The ministry of reconciliation is not assigned to pastors alone or to the learned, but to those who have given their heart to Christ. Your greatest qualification is that you have given your heart to Jesus Christ and you are reconciled with Him. You don't need all the answers to people's questions, just that you know he touched your life and He will touch theirs. This is why you can witness to anyone right now.

2 Corinthians (2Cor) 5:18 And all things [are] of God, who hath reconciled us to himself by Jesus Christ, and hath given to us the ministry of reconciliation;

The Greek word for Reconciled is **καταλλασσω** katallasso (pronounced kat-al-las'-so) which means

> 1) to change, exchange, as coins for others of equivalent value
> 1a) to reconcile (those who are at variance)
> 1b) return to favor with, be reconciled to one
> 1c) to receive one into favor

Not only did Jesus reconcile or return us to favor with God, he gave us the job of helping Him return others to favor! God did this by exchanging His son for our sins. I know this sound like a bad trade but God loves us so much that it was a good deal to Him. He loves mankind that much!

John 3:16 For God so loved the world, that he gave his only begotten Son, that whosoever believeth in him should not perish, but have everlasting life.

God and Jesus didn't wait for mankind to get right before he made the exchange to bring us back into favor!

Rom 5:8 But God commendeth his love toward us, in that, while we were yet sinners, Christ died for us.

This is how we learn to know God, though Jesus, and to know ourselves as God sees us. All we have to do is invite Jesus into our heart. It is that simple!

Feel free to share what God has done for you through Jesus Christ. There are so many lost people that are looking for rest, but don't know what they are looking for. For some, you may be the only messenger of the Good News (the Gospel of Jesus Christ) that they will ever encounter. You may not know all the answers but you know who does; Jesus Christ! I wish I could go back to the young person who first exposed me to the gospel of Jesus Christ. I would hug his neck and thank him for caring enough to share. He planted a seed that took root and has changed my life forever.

Remember that if you are planting seed or watering, you may not get a positive reaction. It takes time for the seed to die and resurrect to spring out of the ground. I remember my response to the seed planted by that faithful sixteen year old, I was underwhelmed by it all. But don't despise the day of small things!

1.11

When Things Go Wrong

Now that you are saved, your life has entered into a realignment stage both spiritually and naturally. Some things in your life that seemed to be easy before salvation may become difficult for you. Some things may just go wrong; seemingly out of nowhere. It is common for things to go wrong when you become a Christian because most of the things you occupied your time with before salvation was provided by God's enemy. Now that you are under new ownership, the enemy, Satan, wants to pull everything out from under you so he can persuade you come back to him. He is hoping that you esteem all his pleasures above your relationship with Jesus. It's a lot like the wilderness experience Jesus went through when He was beginning his ministry. The enemy tried to tempt Jesus with things he thought Jesus esteemed highly.

Matt 4:1 ¶ Then was Jesus led up of the Spirit into the wilderness to be tempted of the devil. **2** And when he had fasted forty days and forty nights, he was afterward an hungred. **3** And when the tempter came to him, he said, If thou be the Son of God, command that these stones be made bread. **4** But he answered and said, **It is written, Man shall not live by bread alone, but by every word that proceedeth out of the mouth of God**. **5** Then the devil taketh him up into the holy city, and setteth him on a pinnacle of the temple, **6** And saith unto him, If thou be the Son of God, cast thyself down: for it is written, He shall give his angels charge concerning thee: and in [their] hands they shall bear thee up, lest at any time thou dash thy foot against a stone. **7** Jesus said unto him, **It is written again, Thou**

shalt not tempt the Lord thy God. 8 Again, the devil taketh him up into an exceeding high mountain, and sheweth him all the kingdoms of the world, and the glory of them; 9 And saith unto him, All these things will I give thee, if thou wilt fall down and worship me. 10 Then saith Jesus unto him, **Get thee hence, Satan: for it is written, Thou shalt worship the Lord thy God, and him only shalt thou serve.** 11 Then the devil leaveth him, and, behold, angels came and ministered unto him.

You see, Jesus showed us how to deal with everything we face as we see the enemy stir up trouble to entice us to turn back. All we have to do is quote the Word of God. For now, you can use versus 4, 7, and 10 until you learn more.

One more weapon at your immediate disposal that you should be aware of; speaking Jesus' name out loud. You see, every time Jesus' name is spoken in a whisper, or with a voice, it provokes a promise from God in the scriptures.

Rom 10:13 For whosoever shall call upon the name of the Lord shall be saved.

Psalms (Ps) 18:3 I will call upon the LORD, [who is worthy] to be praised: so shall I be saved from mine enemies.

When you are dealing with an overwhelming thought, or a situation is pressuring you to choose to do the wrong thing, you can call on Jesus. Maybe you are fighting to respond differently than you have in the past, you might be scared or something tragic is about to unfold, CALL ON JESUS!!!

When you are faced with people who have changed the way they treat you because of your new lifestyle, remember this; if they were at peace with you when you were in the world, then they may have been placed in your life by the enemy to keep you under his influence. Once you come to Christ, that same person will try to put pressure on you to give up this new walk. Don't be fooled! You didn't mean that much to them before! The best way to respond is to tell them quietly that Jesus loves them and so do you. That is all you can do. Making Jesus more important than all else can get you much further in a shorter amount of time than hanging on to something that the enemy is threatening to take.

The Good News is you have a new provider (JESUS) who gives you all that you need with no strings attached right here and right now!

Philippians (Php) 4:19 But my God shall supply all your need according to his riches in glory by Christ Jesus.

So let the enemy take what is his… You no longer need it! God has all the resources anyway. The enemy steels them and tries to make you think he is the owner and the provider. This is a LIE! Here is why:

Ps 24:1 The earth is the Lord's, and the fullness thereof; the world, and they that dwell therein.

God said:

Ps 50:10 For every beast of the forest is mine, and the cattle upon a thousand hills.

You know it comes from God when it does not add sorrow!

Proverbs (Prov) 10:22 The blessing of the Lord, it maketh rich, and addeth no sorrow with it.

You can believe this! You have moved on to a richer King! He has your back and will provide much better for you.

1.12

Dealing with Our Issues

The word of God depicts our hearts as a farmer's field. After letting it grow wild for so many years, some large bushes and trees have established themselves securely in the ground of our heart. Each bush and tree has a different name like Undisciplined, Anger, Impatience, Selfishness, Rudeness, Lusting, Adultery and the list can go on. In order to take control of our heart, Jesus is going to bring us to a specific bush or tree that he wants to remove from the soil of our heart. Be encouraged! He does not show us these to hurt us, but to help us uproot them out of our life. It is very difficult to clear a field in the dark! So we must see what we are to take down.

The larger plant or tree is what I want to address here. You see, walking with Jesus is 95% a development work and 5% deliverance. Although our deliverance or healing is tremendous, wonderful and necessary, what I'm talking about here is a lifestyle that we pursue for the rest of our lives on this earth.

Let's say that the Spirit of God has revealed to us that we have anger in our heart (it could be any sin really). When we see the anger in our heart, Jesus wants to take it away from us; however, he cannot unless we give it to him. We give it to Jesus when we say "**Lord Jesus, forgive me of my anger (don't be afraid to call the sin out by name) and help me to behave and think like you**". When we say that, we cut a branch off of the anger bush or tree. If it is a small plant, we may be able to pull it out by the roots the first time and be done with it. If it is larger, we must cut it down to size before we can uproot it.

Like large bushes and trees, the large issues in our heart must be cut down to a stump, dug around the stump, cut the roots, pull the stump out of the ground, and finally fill the hole. So don't be discouraged if you find yourself asking Jesus to forgive you on the "same thing" over and over again! You are simply cutting it down to a stump. It looks the same because it comes from the same tree **BUT** it is a different branch.

WARNING!

The enemy will try to convince you that this process is not working. "You are not getting any better, why don't you just quit!" This is a clear sign that you are making progress! The enemy is liar. So if a liar tells you something, then the opposite must be true. Besides, there is another reason the enemy wants you to quit!

Like bushes and trees, if we cut a branch off and leave it unattended, 5 to 7 more branches will grow from that cut spot; making the plant fuller, bigger, and stronger. This may explain why those who come to Christ and leave are worse than before; the plants have been pruned and it stimulated growth.

DO NOT STOP CUTTING UNTIL IT IS UPROOTED!

How do you know when you have uprooted it? Simple, you are not dealing with it anymore. After a period of time of having that particular tree gone, we may find another tree of similar kind in the field. Just get out the ax and begin to remove it.

MULTIPLE BUSH AND TREE CUTTING:

In my 33 years of serving Jesus, there have been several times in my walk that I have had to clear a lot of bushes and trees at one time. I admit that it is a time of continual repentance and can be exhausting. As I write this book, I am not currently in this state. However, I know I will return to this phase at some point because this walk has a cycle to it. Giving a life to Jesus takes a lifetime.

Life is a circle, which means that our walk with Jesus has a cycle. We normally start with repenting and clearing land in our hearts, and then there is a season that we till our ground to get it ready to receive good seed. Next we cultivate our plants and trees of Godly traits, and then we glean the fruit of our labor. Finally we return full circle to clearing more land. It is not unusual to be clearing a field, tilling another, cultivate another and glean the fruit of yet another field in our hearts all at once.

Hang in there! You will become proficient as you practice this art of spiritual multitasking. This is what helps us to be a doer of the word and not a hearer only!

James (Jas) 1:22 But be ye doers of the word, and not hearers only, deceiving your own selves.

Welcome to the true life and processes of Christianity! This is a love relationship with Jesus Christ! Along the way He will bless and amaze us at the power and glory He has placed in our life. Remember!!!

1Cor 15:57 But thanks [be] to God, which giveth us the victory through our Lord Jesus Christ.

Rom 8:37 Nay, in all these things we are more than conquerors through him that loved us. **38** For I am persuaded, that neither death, nor life, nor angels, nor principalities, nor powers, nor things present, nor things to come, **39** Nor height, nor depth, nor any other creature, shall be able to separate us from the love of God, which is in Christ Jesus our Lord.

Be encouraged. You are a diamond in the rough. Jesus is cutting and polishing until you become that much desired and beautiful diamond you were meant to be.

1.13

Fasting

Fasting can be a powerful weapon to ward off the attack of your struggles. When fasting, the mind becomes sharper, the heavy bands of the world lighten and you can find relief from so many issues.

Fasting humbles our soul. When our soul is wanting this and that or having emotional fits against our selves, fasting can bring peace.

Ps 35:13 ... I humbled my soul with fasting; ...

For the first three years of my walk with Jesus, I fasted every Monday; no food or water for 24 hrs. Not that you should, I'm just sharing what helped me get above the twenty two years of sinful training.

GOD'S FAST

Isa 58:6 [Is] not this the fast that I have chosen? to loose the bands of wickedness, to undo the heavy burdens, and to let the oppressed go free, and that ye break every yoke? **7** [Is it] not to deal thy bread to the hungry, and that thou bring the poor that are cast out to thy house? when thou seest the naked, that thou cover him; and that thou hide not thyself from thine own flesh? **8** ¶ Then shall thy light break forth as the morning, and thine health shall spring forth speedily: and thy righteousness shall go before thee; the glory of the LORD shall be thy rereward. **9** Then shalt thou call, and the LORD shall answer; thou shalt cry, and he shall say, Here I [am]. If thou take away from the midst of thee the yoke, the putting forth of the finger, and speaking vanity;   **10** And [if] thou draw out thy soul to the hungry, and satisfy the afflicted soul; then shall thy light rise in obscurity, and thy darkness [be] as the noonday: **11** And the LORD shall guide thee continually, and satisfy thy soul in drought, and make fat thy bones: and thou shalt be like a watered garden, and like a spring of water, whose waters fail not.   **12** And [they that shall be] of thee shall build the old waste places: thou shalt raise up the foundations of many generations; and thou shalt be called, The repairer of the breach, The restorer of paths to dwell in. **13** ¶ If thou turn away thy foot from the sabbath, [from] doing thy pleasure on my holy day; and call the sabbath a delight, the holy of the LORD, honourable; and shalt honour him, not doing thine own ways, nor finding thine own pleasure, nor speaking [thine own] words: 14 Then shalt thou delight thyself in the LORD; and I will cause thee to ride upon the high places of the earth, and feed thee with the heritage of Jacob thy father: for the mouth of the LORD hath spoken [it].

When God leads us to fast, we can rest assured that all the benefits mentioned above are bestowed on us. The benefits I am referring to are as follows:

- Loose the bands of wickedness
- Undo heavy burdens
- Let the oppressed go free
- You break every yoke
- Give your bread to the hungry
- Bring the poor that are cast out to your house
- Clothe the naked
- We don't hide ourselves from our own sin

Yes, all these benefits are blessings on dimensions beyond our comprehension. God being a balanced God, He mentions spiritual and natural blessings. He also mentions spiritual things that we should do as well as physical.

In doing these things for a fast, God makes the following promises:

- Your light will break forth as the morning.
- Your health will improve speedily.
- Your righteousness will go before you.
- You will receive the glory of the Lord as a Re-Reward.
- The Lord will answer your call to Him.
- The Lord will guide you continually.
- The Lord will satisfy your soul in drought and make fat your bones.
- You shall be like a watered garden.
- You shall be like a water spring that never runs dry.
- Your family shall restore the loss in your life.
- You will strengthen your foundations for many generations.
- You will be known as the repairer of the breach, the restorer of paths to dwell in.
- You will delight in the Lord.
- God will cause you to ride on the high places of the earth.
- You will be fed with the heritage of Jacob.

Fasting is very dynamic and cannot be overlooked. It is important that we have a regular practice of fasting.

The contract here is in exchange for fasting. If I go to the store and purchase some bananas, I exchange legal tender for the fruit. This can be considered a contract. To add bread to the shopping, I must exchange legal tender again. This is what I mean when I say that fasting is a contract between you and God. God will keep His end of the contract; just fast. You may need to start by skipping a meal once in a while. Some can jump right into a full 24 hour fast. You decide what is best for you. Don't allow your attempts to fast to become legalistic. If you start a fast and don't complete your predetermined time, don't let it bother you. I have broken more fasts than I have completed; just keep at it because you are still making progress. I fasted because I was seeking liberty from my issues. If you are struggling with your issues, fasting may be the answer for you.

JESUS' INSTRUCTIONS ON HOW TO FAST

Jesus gave us some instructions on how to fast properly:

Matt 6:16 ¶ Moreover when ye fast, be not, as the hypocrites, of a sad countenance: for they disfigure their faces, that they may appear unto men to fast. Verily I say unto you, They have their reward. **17** But thou, when thou fastest, anoint thine head, and wash thy face; **18** That thou appear not unto men to fast, but unto thy Father which is in secret: and thy Father, which seeth in secret, shall reward thee openly.

Sometimes when fasting, someone offers you some food. You don't want to tell people that you are fasting but you don't want to be rude either. It is OK to tell the person who is offering you food that you are fasting. And it is OK if you tell them that you are not hungry. The Lord sees that you are not trying to make a show of it and will bless you anyway.

We can be happy when we fast. If you are fasting and feel tired, try doing a few jumping jacks or pushups. Exercise actually helps us feel stronger. If you are medically challenged to fast, pray and ask the Lord what you can do without for a period of time to enter into this powerful covenant. Like all things, the more you practice fasting, the better you get at it.

Fasting also helps with the battleground of the mind which is the next subject.

1.14

The Battleground of the Mind

Don't be alarmed at your thoughts! Now that you are saved, the Holy Ghost is waging war against all thoughts that are not of God. Some of these thoughts are from your training in the past, some from other people's suggestive words, some are from the untamed portion of your heart, and some are from the enemy.

All battles start and finish here. Your actions and words are the result of the thought that has predominance.

2 Cor 10:3 For though we walk in the flesh, we do not war after the flesh: **4** (For the weapons of our warfare [are] not carnal, but mighty through God to the pulling down of strong holds;) **5 Casting down imaginations, and every high thing that exalteth itself against the knowledge of God, and bringing into captivity every thought to the obedience of Christ;**

Every time we are caught up in a thought that is not of God, no matter how strong, we can break its hold by just calling on the name of Jesus with our voice. We will cover the power of the spoken word more in another section.

Rom 10:13 For whosoever shall call upon the name of the Lord shall be saved.

I have learned to call on Jesus' name for uncontrollable thoughts, close calls in traffic, confusion at my job, conflict in my house and many other things. He has delivered me out of them all! This is how we do battle! So practice with this new weapon so that you can gain confidence in its strength and power!

Another way to establish a better thought-life is by committing your works to the Lord.

Prov 16:3 ¶ Commit thy works unto the LORD, and thy thoughts shall be established.

Here the Hebrew word for Works is מעשה ma'aseh (pronounced mah-as-eh') meaning: work, needlework, acts, labor, doing, art, deed, a thing done, business, pursuit, undertaking, enterprise, achievement, a thing made, and product.

As you can see, when we commit our works to Jesus and do things for Him, He gives us the victory over our thoughts.
So ensure that you are doing something for the Lord so that He can help you take the reins of your thoughts and direct them to Godly things.

Php 4:7 And the peace of God, which passeth all understanding, **shall keep your hearts and minds through Christ Jesus**. **8** Finally, brethren, whatsoever things are true, whatsoever things [are] honest, whatsoever things [are] just, whatsoever things [are] pure, whatsoever things [are] lovely, whatsoever things [are] of good report; if [there be] any virtue, and if [there be] any praise, **think on these things**.

Philippians 4:7-8 show us that God wants us to be victorious in our mind and gives us a rule to measure our thoughts. Here we can know what is acceptable to Jesus. Remember, He knows our thoughts so let's cast down those thoughts that are not pleasing to Jesus by calling His name and doing a work for Him to break the stronghold.

1.15

God Corrects Those Whom He Loves

I have two beautiful children. When they were very young I needed to play the role of trainer. This meant that I needed to use every opportunity to teach them principles and show them what was right and wrong. This included pointing out things that weren't very pleasant to see. They are adults now and I don't play that role any longer. However, God is all things to us and at times must show us things about ourselves that we don't always want to see.

God's motivation in showing us difficult things about ourselves is to begin the changing process. Just as it is difficult to clean a room in the dark, it is difficult to clean a room in the mansion of our heart without seeing what is wrong. The beautiful thing about this is that immediately Jesus provides a solution while we discover something that is not right in our heart. He brings the solution to the problem. All this is done in Love. You are a son of God. I cannot put this any better than the scripture:

Heb 12:5 And ye have forgotten the exhortation which speaketh unto you as unto children, My son, despise not thou the chastening of the Lord, nor faint when thou art rebuked of him: **6** For whom the Lord loveth he chasteneth, and scourgeth every son whom he receiveth. **7** If ye endure chastening, God dealeth with you as with sons; for what son is he whom the father chasteneth not? **8** But if ye be without chastisement, whereof all are partakers, then are ye bastards, and not sons. **9** Furthermore we have had fathers of our flesh which corrected [us], and we gave [them] reverence: shall we not much rather be in subjection unto the Father of spirits, and live? **10** For they verily for a few days chastened [us] after their own pleasure; but he for [our] profit, that [we] might be partakers of his holiness. **12** Wherefore lift up the hands which hang down, and the feeble knees; **13** And make straight paths for your feet, lest that which is lame be turned out of the way; but let it rather be healed.

As already stated, correction is not easy but needful. Verse 7 is conditional; you must choose to endure to be dealt with as a son by God. A son has more access to the things of God than a servant. Verse 10 tells us why God chastens us; for our profit. He desires for us to profit all in all.

When we find ourselves corrected by the Lord, we simply need to ask for forgiveness and press on with Jesus. So if you are overwhelmed by the struggle of your issues, thoughts and correction of the Lord, call on Jesus' name for relief. He will answer.

Remember that this process, though difficult at times, severs the ties and influence the world has upon you. When we run to Jesus in the tough times we are denying ourselves and taking up our cross.

Matt 16:24 ¶ Then said Jesus unto his disciples, If any [man] will come after me, let him deny himself, and take up his cross, and follow me.

Be encouraged! This season shall pass; as all do.

Rom 8:37 Nay, in all these things we are more than conquerors through him that loved us. 38 For I am persuaded, that neither death, nor life, nor angels, nor principalities, nor powers, nor things present, nor things to come,**39** Nor height, nor depth, nor any other creature, shall be able to separate us from the love of God, which is in Christ Jesus our Lord.

So whenever you see something ungodly about yourself, your change starts by saying "forgive me Lord".

God's first choice is to deal with you privately (in your prayer closet; in secret). When we stay honest with God and repent as we see sin, this is as far as it goes.

The following scripture describes God hiding mysteries and a king able to search them out. However, I believe that the first segment is also a revelation of the nature of God. He does not try to get glory by publicly exposing sin. It is His glory to cover our sins privately.

Prov 25:2 ¶ [It is] the glory of God to conceal a thing: but the honour of kings [is] to search out a matter.

Having our sins publicly exposed is shameful. God said that if we wait for Him, we will not be ashamed.

Isa 49:23 And kings shall be thy nursing fathers, and their queens thy nursing mothers: they shall bow down to thee with [their] face toward the earth, and lick up the dust of thy feet; **and thou shalt know that I [am] the LORD: for they shall not be ashamed that wait for me.**

When we stop waiting on the Lord in prayer and stop allowing Him to correct us privately, then we become vulnerable to public exposure. This is where I believe the balance lies between Prov25:2a and Prov27:5.

Prov27:5 ¶ Open rebuke [is] better than secret love.

God loves us too much to let us slide with our flaws.

1.16

Money; God's Way

When I first found out about giving to the Lord, I was angry because no one shared this principle with me sooner. Here I was, trying to battle my way for Jesus and I could have been entering into a covenant with Him that may have saved me some effort. So if you are like me, you will be glad that I added this section in.

SPIRITUAL FIRST, THEN NATURAL

God is a Spirit who created the natural heavens and the earth. We existed in the spirit realm before we arrived on earth. The spirit always precedes the natural. With that, you will understand when I tell you that we are spiritual beings having a natural experience. Everything about our lives is founded by the spirit first then manifests in the natural world.

So it makes sense that when we deal with money and creating wealth, we must attend to the spiritual first and then work with the natural. Any other order will not succeed. It is also vitally important that we, as Christians, operate in the same manner as our Father who has made us in His image and likeness.

The world teaches that money is everything. The truth is, money is not everything, it is simply a tool. If we know how to use it, it will help us. If we don't know how to use it, then we may become frustrated and fail at trying to reach our financial goals.

When we join the family of God by asking Jesus Christ into our heart, we entered a new realm of financial principles. Now, when we engage in financial projects, we must do it God's way to ensure success.

As Christians, our true success in our walk now and forever is directly related to our ability to live spiritually AND naturally. God created this world to be inhabited with prosperity from all dimensions. He wants us to prosper in our Spirit, Soul and Body. Our goal is to prosper in all three dimensions. The bottom line here is that God is not satisfied with only your spirit prospering; He wants your body and soul to prosper as well. This is God's idea of balance.

3 John (3Joh) 1:2 Beloved, I wish above all things that thou mayest prosper and be in health, even as thy soul prospereth.

1 Thessalonians (1 Thes) 5:23 ¶ And the very God of peace sanctify you wholly; and [I pray God] your whole spirit and soul and body be preserved blameless unto the coming of our Lord Jesus Christ.

God wants to make a show of it! This is how He proves to the world how great He really is. This is why God has given us instructions on how to prosper on all facets of our life. When a Christian prospers before a desperate wanting world, it is evident that Jesus Christ is a real solution. However, we must do our part to cooperate with the word of God.

1 Timothy (1Tim) 4:15 Meditate upon these things; give thyself wholly to them; **that thy profiting may appear to all. 16** Take heed unto thyself, and unto the doctrine; continue in them: for in doing this thou shalt both save thyself, and them that hear thee.

Mark 16:17 And these signs shall follow them that believe; In my name shall they cast out devils; they shall speak with new tongues; **18** They shall take up serpents; and if they drink any deadly thing, it shall not hurt them; they shall lay hands on the sick, and they shall recover.

The two scriptures above point out that God is a demonstrative God. He manifests in all dimensions and makes His presence known. Jesus is a very present help in time of need.

Ps 46:1 ¶ «To the chief Musician for the sons of Korah, A Song upon Alamoth.» God [is] our refuge and strength, a very present help in trouble.

GOD'S PLAN IS TO DO AWAY WITH POVERTY

In the middle of directing the Israelites on releasing the debt of their brothers after seven years, God reveals his plan to bless them so much that poverty would no longer exist with them.

Deuteronomy (Deu) 15:4 Save when there shall be no poor among you; for the LORD shall greatly bless thee in the land which the LORD thy God giveth thee [for] an inheritance to possess it:

The word Save in Hebrew is אפס 'ephec (pronounced eh'-fes) meaning: ceasing, end, finality. Clearly God reveals His plan to abolish poverty.

Now that we are graphed into the tree of the Israelites, God's plan to eradicate poverty includes us.

Rom 11:16 For if the firstfruit [be] holy, the lump [is] also [holy]: and if the root [be] holy, so [are] the branches. **17** And if some of the branches be broken off, and thou, being a wild olive tree, wert graffed in among them, and with them partakest of the root and fatness of the olive tree;

In Romans 11 above, Paul is describing Israel as the first fruit and an olive tree. He is also describing the gentiles who are saved by Jesus Christ as a wild olive tree being graphed into the olive tree and partaking of the root and fatness of the tree. This is why we Christians can claim the favor and benefits that God provides to the Israelites. It is His financial structure, as we apply it, that causes us to have victory over poverty.

ENTERING INTO SIX CONTRACTS WITH GOD

The word of God gives us direction on how to prosper in all dimensions. In this section, we will be covering the financial aspect. When I go to the store and purchase laundry detergent, I give an agreed amount of money in exchange for the product. This is considered a contract between me and the store; simple, but still a contract. If I decide to purchase an additional item, I enter into an additional contract to exchange another agreed amount of money for the additional item. This principle originated from God.

There are six principles God has given us that allows us to prosper financially. These principles are financial contracts that provide different functions. **These contracts must be done together to achieve maximum prosperity. Separately, they are unable to provide the complete success that God has for you.** Incidentally, the very reason why the Jewish people are prosperous today is because they practice these six contracts as a way of life.

Your goal is to make a plan to phase into working these contracts. I highly recommend starting with contract #1 and working to implement all six in the order that they are numbered, however it is a given that you will be operating #6 while making your changes.

Also note that there are three Spiritual Contracts and three Natural Contracts. These contracts are:

1. Tithes ~ Spiritual Contract
2. First Fruits ~ Spiritual Contract
3. Offering ~ Spiritual Contract
4. Emergency Fund ~ Natural Contract
5. Retirement Fund ~ Natural Contract
6. Living Expenses ~ Natural Contract

Jeremiah (Jer) 29:11 For I know the thoughts that I think toward you, saith the LORD, thoughts of peace, and not of evil, to give you an expected end.

God's expected end is greater than we can imagine. We must enter into all six of these contracts with Him to see the wonder of our true destiny that He has planned.

The way we handle our resources must follow spiritual and natural principles for our greatest benefit. Your time, talent, gifts, possessions and money are your resources. This section will cover how to apply your money to achieve your greatest advantage.

Money is a tool and like a computer, car, and chair; if we do not know how to use it, we will not gain the greatest benefit from it, and may hurt ourselves.

MY TESTAMONY

The following formulas came from a unique situation that I found myself having to deal with. I was pastoring a church that was in transition and in between pastors. A woman came to the church that was pregnant, with two toddlers and her husband was in jail. What's worse, she didn't have a place to stay, no money, food or job. We quickly got her into the government's system that provided a place to stay, utilities and food. Then we helped her get a job. Once completed, I felt that we had done nothing to help her become independent from the system. So I prayed and asked God to show me how to teach her and others how to come out of this poverty state.

God answered me in spades. Until then, I had not realized that He had a vendetta against poverty! He also showed me that these contracts were provided to help those who are in need to come out with abundance. It is these six contracts that the Lord has shown me as His divine financial plan.

Let's look at the six contracts that will revolutionize your life and enable you to prosper like you never thought possible.

TITHES & FIRSTFRUITS

Like others, I thought that first fruits and tithes were the same thing until I came upon this scripture.

2 Chronicles (2Chr) 31:5 And as soon as the commandment came abroad, the children of Israel brought in abundance the **firstfruits** of corn, wine, and oil, and honey, and of all the increase of the field; **and the tithe** of all [things] brought they in abundantly.

When God states "first fruits and tithes", it's like going to the grocery store and getting bread and butter. I have them both, but they are different items. After studying the two, I realized that they provided two totally different functions or benefits. First Fruits is the first ripened fruit in the field, while the tithe is ten percent of all the harvest.

1. TITHES CONTRACT ~ Spiritual

Malachi (Mal)3:10 Bring ye all the tithes into the storehouse, that there may be meat in mine house, and prove me now herewith, saith the LORD of hosts, if I will not open you the windows of heaven, and pour you out a blessing, that [there shall] not [be room] enough [to receive it]. **11** And I will rebuke the devourer for your sakes, and he shall not destroy the fruits of your ground; neither shall your vine cast her fruit before the time in the field, saith the LORD of hosts. **12** And all nations shall call you blessed: for ye shall be a delightsome land, saith the LORD of hosts.

This contract brings four spiritual benefits that we need to prosper naturally.

❖ Open Up The Windows of Heaven ~ If the windows of heaven are shut in our life, we can never reach our destiny.

❖ Pour You Out A Blessing, that there will not be room enough to receive it ~ We need His abundance to exceed our expectations

❖ Rebuke the Devourer for your sakes, and he shall not destroy the Fruits of your ground ~ Things last longer and our efforts are not wasted.

❖ Your vine will not cast her fruit before the time in the field ~ The product of our work will be in perfect timing; the right place at the right time.

Tithes in the Hebrew comes from the word מעשׂר ma'aser (pronounced mah-as-ayr') meaning: .1, tenth part, or 10%. When we bring our tithes into the church, it will be ten percent of our gross income (before taxes are taken out). To calculate how much that would be, we multiply our gross income by .1.

I recommend implementing this contract as soon as possible.

2. FIRST FRUIT CONTRACT ~ Spiritual

Exodus (Ex) 23:19 The first of the firstfruits of thy land thou shalt bring into the house of the LORD thy God. Thou shalt not seethe a kid in his mother's milk. **20** ¶ Behold, I send an Angel before thee, to keep thee in the way, and to bring thee into the place which I have prepared.**21** Beware of him, and obey his voice, provoke him not; for he will not pardon your transgressions: for my name [is] in him.

This promise of an angel to lead the Israelites into their promise land took place well after the pillar of fire by night and cloud by day lead them across the Red Sea. They had already received the Ten Commandments and began to build the tabernacle. My point is that this angel is an additional blessing. Our experience of the Holy Ghost that leads and guides us into all truth is the New Testament manifestation of when Israel was being lead by the pillar of cloud and fire in the wilderness. The promise of an Angel to go before us is an additional blessing when we give our first fruits. This angel, mentioned in verse 20 above, had a distinct difference in that its purpose is to bring us into our individual destiny. I believe the leading of the angel here is different than the Holy Ghost because it will lead us into our promise land of destiny that we would normally miss.

This contract provides a spiritual promise with instructions for us to follow.

❖ <u>God will send an Angel in front of you</u> ~ this angel will block unseen obstacles waiting to hinder your progress; or distract you from your destiny.

❖ <u>Be aware of His presence and purpose</u> ~ In order to follow the angel, we must be cognizant of his presence and understand that he is to guide us into God's plan for our life.

❖ <u>Obey his voice</u> ~ We will hear his voice leading us to do the right thing. He will encourage us to trust God that He will take care of the things out of our control. By obeying His voice, we will find ourselves in the right place at the right time. We will produce and release ideas at the exact moment to bring the most return.

To determine how much should be given for a first fruit, we must look at the predominant source of income during that time; which was farming. This principle holds true today. If you were to plant a field, 1/40th, 2.5% or .025 will ripen first and must be harvested earlier than the rest of the crop. In farming, this 2.5% is considered the first fruits. To calculate how much that would be you simply multiply your gross income by .025.

3. OFFERING CONTRACT ~ Spiritual

Luke 6:38 Give, and it shall be given unto you; good measure, pressed down, and shaken together, and running over, shall men give into your bosom. For with the same measure that ye mete withal it shall be measured to you again.

Many offerings were made in the Mosaic Tabernacle for many purposes. The free will offering is the one that we see represented here. There is no mandatory amount to be given; just that you give with a cheerful heart. This is from your relationship with God.

This contract will cause people to give to us:

- ❖ Good Measure ~ more than fair in return.

- ❖ Pressed Down ~ compacted and concentrated.

- ❖ Shaken Together ~ to allow for more to be put in.

- ❖ Running Over ~ spilling out of your ability to contain it.

Again, this is an amount that you alone decide to give. For the sake of a number, I use 3% or .03. I multiply my gross income by .03 to determine the amount of my offering. Just remember that this contract causes provisions to come running after you!

Remember that you are spiritual first and then natural. The most effective process for Christians to operate is from who you are in the order of precedence. The spiritual will always take precedence over the natural. God is a God of eternal plans; He chooses to work with the part of you that is eternal. Additionally, as Christians, we are guaranteed financial success when we operate according to God's priority.

Due to the unpredictability of LIFE, our spiritual contracts protect our efforts in the natural contracts.

4. EMERGENCY FUND CONTRACT ~ Natural

This contract provides a buffer for the happenings of life. With the spiritual contracts in place, this contract will be more than enough to help you for those unexpected issues that we all face. Proverbs speaks about the ant that stores away food to provide when there is lack. Building an emergency fund is a very spiritual act (although a Natural Contract) because you are doing as the word of God directs.

Prov 6:6 ¶ Go to the ant, thou sluggard; consider her ways, and be wise: **7** Which having no guide, overseer, or ruler, **8** Provideth her meat in the summer, [and] gathereth her food in the harvest.

Purpose: This is for LIFE. To help us prepare for unexpected things so that we do not get overwhelmed by them.

Goal: The Emergency Fund needs to be built up to 6 months of pay in a separate bank account. This money must be available for withdrawal in one day in an emergency. In the event you lose your job, you have enough to carry you while you seek another. If you use any of this money, you must begin to restore it to 6 months of pay as soon as you can.

I recommend at least 3% of your income go towards building this fund. Once you have reached 6 months, move the 3% to your 30 year money account until you need to replenish the fund again.

5. 30 YEAR MONEY (Retirement) CONTRACT ~ Natural

With the spiritual contracts in place, this contract is protected from the devourer who seeks those unprotected ones and devours their progress; leaving them in discouragement and ruin.

Create another separate account that you can regularly deposit money. This must be an interest bearing account. Try to find a bank that will pay the best interest for your money. It does not matter if there is a penalty for withdrawing the money early or that it takes several days to withdrawal because you are not going to touch it anyway for 30 years or when you retire; whichever comes first.

Purpose: To provide income for the rest of your life by earning interest. At the end of 30 years of contributing, the principle amount will be large enough for you to live off of the interest earned only. This ensures that you will not run out of money should you live longer than you expect.

Goal: I recommend 10% of everything you earn be put into this account for the rest of your life. You do not touch this money until 30 years have passed or when you retire. Even if you are on the streets, you do not touch this money.

This concept is very powerful. For example, if you put $100 a month away, at 8% annual percentage rate, you would have saved the following:

5yrs	$7,247.69
10yrs	$17,766.08
15yrs	$33,524.83
30yrs	$140, 444.09

The interest earned at 30 years would be **<u>$1,036.96 a month for the rest of your life.</u>** Now you have money earning you money. This is the best employee you could ever hire. It is never late, never makes excuses and doesn't have any overhead. I used a simple amortization table at a fixed amount. If you consider that you will experience increase as you continue in your contracts with God, you could easily create a monthly income of $3,000 a month on interest alone.

FUTURE GENERATIONS

Prov 13:22 ¶ A good [man] leaveth an inheritance to his children's children: and the wealth of the sinner [is] laid up for the just.

This inheritance speaks of teaching your family to love Jesus Christ, how to make a living, these six contracts and passing on possessions and money to the next generations.

Teach your children to do this same principle. If you make it mandatory, by the time they have done this for ten years, they will see the effects and will not stop. I recommend that you keep three piggy banks; one for the Emergency Fund, 30 year Money and Spending. Once the amounts reach $100 or so, you can open up three accounts for them as a teaching aid and for them to see the benefits of it all. These can be simple accounts until the 30 year Money is enough to invest in CDs or better interest bearing accounts.

When you pass, you will leave an inheritance of money AND the knowledge of how to gain wealth to your children whom you will require that they teach this principle to their children as well. While you live off of the interest earned only, wealth will build on wealth as the inheritance is passed on that will change your generations to come dramatically.

Let's work through a scenario:

You put away $100 a month with 3% APR for 30 Years. You live off the interest earned only. You then pass on the principle to your children and they duplicate the same.

1st Generation ~ You

> Total Savings: $103,690.84
> Monthly Interest Earned: $259.23

2nd Generation ~ Your Children

> Total Savings: $691,886.86
> Monthly Interest Earned: $1,729.72

3rd Generation ~ Your Grand Children

> Total Savings: $4,031,739.95
> Monthly Interest Earned: $10,079.35

4th Generation ~ Your Great Grand Children

> Total Savings: $22,995,857.95
> Monthly Interest Earned: $57,489.64

This four generation plan will take approximately 60 years.

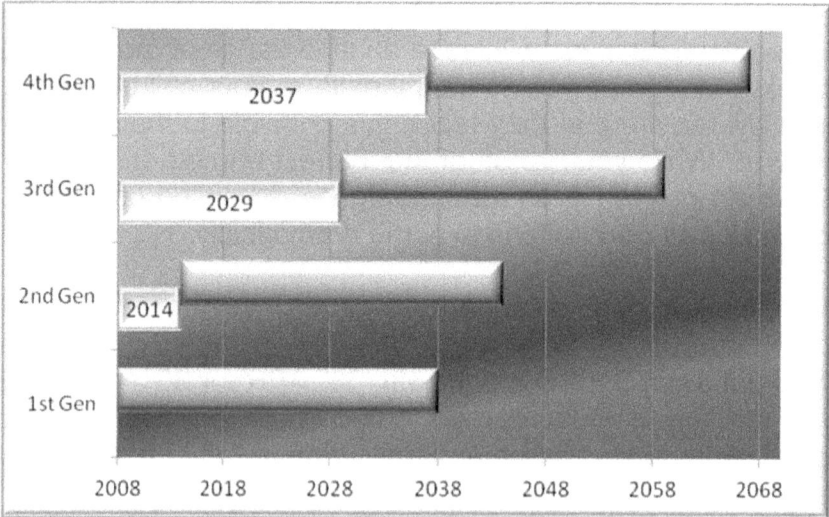

FIGURE 1. Generational Timeline.

NOTE: My future son-in-law is a banker, he stated that my numbers are very conservative and the industry uses 8% APR for forecasting.

There are many factors that would increase the value that I did not include such as:
- Pay raises
- Contribution increases
- Contributing more than 30 years for the generations that started early in life
- Greater than 3% APR interest earned

Now let's look at the final contract: Living Expenses.

6. LIVING EXPENSES ~ Natural

This contract is protected by the spiritual contracts already in place. The enemy cannot devour this resource that will be required for your everyday living expenses. This portion of your money covers paying for items such as;

Taxes
House
Land
Food
Clothes
Electricity
Water
Garbage/Sewer
Medical Expenses
Car
School Tuition
Toys
Tools
Gifts
Helping Family Members and Others
And any other thing that you desire

	Multiply the Income By:	Amount	
Tithes	0.100	$	-
Offering	0.030	$	-
First Fruits	0.025	$	-
Emergency Fund	0.030	$	-
30 Yr Old Money	0.100	$	-
Living Expensenses	0.715	$	-
Total %	100.00%	$	-

Enter Your Income Here:

Tithes: God's promise to open the windows of Heaven and rebuke the devourer for you. **Mal 3: 10-12**	
Offering: Jesus said "Give and it shall be given to you, good measure, pressed down, shaken together and running over will men give to you." **Luke 6: 38**	Spiritual Contract with God
First Fruits: God's promise to send an Angel in front of us to keep us in the way and to bring us into the place God has prepared for us. **Ex 23: 19-23**	
Emergency Fund: In an account that you can draw the money in the same day. Build to 6 months of pay. **Pr 6:6-8**	
30 Yr Old Money: Put in an intrest earning account. DO NOT TOUCH! Until 30 yrs of saving or retired; whichever comes first. Live off of the interest earned only. **Pr 13:22**	Natural Contract with God
Living Expenses : Pays for Taxes, House, Land, Cars, Tuition, Clothes, Utilities, Food, and anything else. .	

FIGURE 2. God's Financial Plan.

Figure 2 shows you how to compute the proper biblical and recommended amounts. Feel free to copy the Figure and keep in your wallet.

BUYING A CAR

How would you like to be able to buy the car of your dreams cash? Here is how you do it:

Let's say that you are still making payments of $300 a month on your current car. Once you have finished all the payments, you must keep your car for 5 more years. During the next five years, put $300 away in an interest bearing account as your new car account. At the end of five years, you will have $18, 614.21 (Simple Interest of 2% APR).

Now if you buy a two to three year old car from a dealer with the money saved, you get a car that:
- is practically brand new
- you don't have to pay the new car price
- the kinks have been worked out by the previous owner for you (less chance of taking time to get warranty work done)
- should last you for the next ten years

Do not over spend. This type of pre-owned vehicle is capable of going ten more years. You continue to put $300 a month away for your next car. At the end of ten years, you will have saved $38,785.01. Again buy a 2 or 3 year old car and take this one 15 years. A properly maintained car can last 15 years easy. At the end of $300 a month for fifteen years, you will have saved $61,403.38.

As you can see, this process saves you a lot of money and allows you to increase in the quality of cars you drive. If you don't spend all of your car money, consider saving it for the next car or putting it in your retirement money.

I don't recommend taking a car past 20 years of age because of all the plastics (they tend to dry rot) that are now being used. I took one of my cars to 20 and it performed pretty well. I have another car approaching 15years and it is performing well also.

LOANING MONEY

A side thought on loaning money. If you decide to loan money to another, this money must come from your Living Expenses. If you are not already wealthy, I recommend that you do not loan money, rather, if you can give it away, then do so. Many relationships have been broken over an unpaid loan. However, money given away has blessed some relationships. If you cannot give it away then most likely you do not have the money to loan to anyone. Please remember that you are not God. He is the one who provides all our needs according to His riches in glory. If you cannot help someone monetarily, you can pray with them and ask ministering angels to direct them to receive their Godly need.

Php 4:19 But my God shall supply all your need according to his riches in glory by Christ Jesus.

God is not going to give you money so you can destroy yourself. In a sense, He denies us the resources until we begin to discipline our habits with money. Accountability to God will always be required. With that said, you have a right to know what the money is being spent on if you are providing the funds. If they don't tell you, you should not give the money. Your money is God's money and if you give God's money to someone else, you are responsible for how it was used. If people are in need, most churches write a check to the business rather than giving money. If they are hungry, they are given food not money. If they are behind in their car payment, write a check to the loan company. This prevents God's money from enabling someone to do something with the money that God would not approve of.

Additionally, if they are behind in their bills because of poor money management, you should teach them this information. So find out why before you give.

I feel obligated to teach someone how to manage their finances if I give them money. Money spent is no longer useful. However, information on how to prosper financially can make a poor man prosperous.

FINAL WARNING:

This process is designed by God to be done entirely. If you neglect the spiritual side of Tithing, First Fruits, and Offerings, you put your natural work of Emergency Fund, 30 Year Money and Living Expenses in jeopardy of being devoured by the enemy.

This plan gives us a way to allow the Lord to direct our steps to achieve them.

Prov 16:9 A man's heart deviseth his way: but the LORD directeth his steps.

The Hebrew word for Deviseth is חשׁב chashab (pronounced khaw-shab') meaning: to think, plan, esteem, calculate, invent, make a judgment, imagine, count. God wants us to have a plan in place so that He can direct our steps towards success. By having this plan in place, or as you work towards implementing this plan (spiritual first, then natural), God will direct your steps for you to succeed. So as you begin to apply this plan, He sees your efforts and blesses you.

HOW AM I SUPPOSED TO LIVE OFF OF THIS PLAN?

I am glad that you asked. Once you enter into each of the spiritual contracts, you obligate God to provide for you. Jesus said:

Matt 6:25 ¶ Therefore I say unto you, Take no thought for your life, what ye shall eat, or what ye shall drink; nor yet for your body, what shall ye put on. Is not the life more than meat, and the body than raiment? **26** Behold the fowls of the air: for they sow not, neither do they reap, nor gather into barns; yet your heavenly Father feedeth them. Are ye not much better than they? **27** Which of you by taking thought can add one cubit unto his stature? **28** And why take ye thought for raiment? Consider the lilies of the field, how they grow; they toil not, neither do they spin: 29 And yet I say unto you, That even Solomon in all his glory was not arrayed like one of these. **30** Wherefore, if God so clothe the grass of the field, which today is, and tomorrow is cast into the oven, [shall he] not much more [clothe] you, O ye of little faith? **31** Therefore take no thought, saying, What shall we eat? or, What shall we drink? or, Wherewithal shall we be clothed? **32** (For after all these things do the Gentiles seek:) for your heavenly Father knoweth that ye have need of all these things. **33 But seek ye first the kingdom of God, and his righteousness; and all these things shall be added unto you.** **34** Take therefore no thought for the morrow: for the morrow shall take thought for the things of itself. Sufficient unto the day [is] the evil thereof.

It is His ability to provide for you that enables you to implement this plan. However, you must implement the spiritual contracts first. I recommend gradually working into it if you cannot commit to all six contracts at once. Start with the tithes on the spiritual side and the 30 year money and living expenses on the natural side. Once you have those established, work towards the offering and emergency fund.

Finally, establish the first fruits. You can approach this in any order you like.

MY TESTAMONY

Do you remember my testimony about the woman on page 66, who came to the church in great need? I gave her this formula and she committed to following it. One year later she calls me to ask if I would help her buy a used car for cash. Five years later, she tells me that she no longer qualifies for government assistance because she makes too much money and has too much in the bank! Praise the Lord! I then realized that if it worked for her, that it would work for me and others. So I began to rearrange my priorities and now am seeing God do what He does best; proves Himself a mighty King on behalf of those who trust him!

2Chr 16:9 For the eyes of the LORD run to and fro throughout the whole earth, to shew himself strong in the behalf of [them] whose heart [is] perfect toward him...

We serve a **Living** God! He loves us so much. We can reap the benefits of His love in our Spirit, Soul, and Body to include His provisions. You are not in this alone when you enter into the spiritual contracts with God. God will not allow you to put Him in debt, so He will do what He says He will do. The question is, will you trust in Him?

FROM FAITH TO FAITH

Rom 1:17 For therein is the righteousness of God revealed from faith to faith: as it is written, The just shall live by faith.

Some of you are in financial trouble and cannot see how you could possibly do this right now. My recommendation is that you start off with tithing first. Once your faith in the scriptures concerning tithes is established, move on to the offerings, then first fruits, emergency fund, and finally 30 year old money. Your faith will grow from one faith level to the next.

My wife and I have trusted God to provide many times in our walk and have always brought our tithes into the church. He has never failed us. At that time, the tithe was all we knew. Now that we have a revelation of the other contracts and are walking in them, we are astounded at the results! You will be also. I want to end this section with a few scriptures to remind you of His promises:

Ps 34:10 The young lions do lack, and suffer hunger: but they that seek the LORD shall not want any good [thing].

Matt 6:33 But seek ye first the kingdom of God, and his righteousness; and all these things shall be added unto you.

1.17

The King's Reputation Is At Stake!

Jesus, our King of kings, has promised to be with us.

Heb 13:5 [Let your] conversation [be] without covetousness; [and be] content with such things as ye have: for he hath said, **I will never leave thee, nor forsake thee. 6** So that we may boldly say, The Lord [is] my helper, and I will not fear what man shall do unto me.

As our King, we can take more comfort that he will take care of us. God is not broke down or unable to provide. In fact, He delights in taking care of His subjects.

2Chr 16:9 For the eyes of the LORD run to and fro throughout the whole earth, to shew himself strong in the behalf of [them] whose heart [is] perfect toward him…

To whom does the Lord show himself strong? The answer is to the world of unbelievers! He blesses His people, you and I, to show the world that He is a good provider and to be desired much more than the world.

In a Kingdom, everything belongs to the king to include the subjects. He is responsible for all that is his. This applies to our King Jesus. We Christians are His subjects and we reflect what kind of King He is.

The late Dr. Myles Monroe, pastor of Bahamas Faith Ministries International, has the most dynamic teaching of living in the kingdom of God as a colony on earth. He also teaches this message on YouTube, "Understanding God's

Plan". One of his teachings covers how the kings compete with each other. They compare themselves and their kingdom to other kings and their kingdom. For example, if a king has joyous, healthy, rich, well dressed, and housed subjects, he looks much better than a king who has hopeless, starving, homeless, poor subjects. We see this principle in place when the queen of Sheba comes to test King Solomon.

2Ch 9:1 ¶ And when the queen of Sheba heard of the fame of Solomon, she came to prove Solomon with hard questions at Jerusalem, with a very great company, and camels that bare spices, and gold in abundance, and precious stones: and when she was come to Solomon, she communed with him of all that was in her heart. **2** And Solomon told her all her questions: and there was nothing hid from Solomon which he told her not. **3 And when the queen of Sheba had seen** the wisdom of Solomon, and **the house that he had built, 4 And the meat of his table, and the sitting of his servants, and the attendance of his ministers, and their apparel; his cupbearers also, and their apparel**; and his ascent by which he went up into the house of the LORD; there was no more spirit in her. **5** And she said to the king, [It was] a true report which I heard in mine own land of thine acts, and of thy wisdom: **6 Howbeit I believed not their words, until I came, and mine eyes had seen [it]**: and, behold, the one half of the greatness of thy wisdom was not told me: [for] thou exceedest the fame that I heard. **7** Happy [are] thy men, and happy [are] these thy servants, which stand continually before thee, and hear thy wisdom.

Notice that her determination was not on the King alone but on the welfare of his servants as well. She observes his provision on the table, the way the ministers attended to him in honor, and their clothing. She then comments on the countenance of his servants and his men. They were happy to be continually before him to hear his wisdom. Jesus wants us to be happy to continually be before Him to hear His wisdom. This wisdom produces results! So why wouldn't we be happy to be before Him.

Now I could discuss our behavior here but I will cover the fact that King Jesus wants to look better than all other kings to include His arch enemy Lucifer.

So if you have a need, call on Jesus your King and ask Him to provide for His subject (you). This is why Jesus receives all the praise; He takes care of His own. He will not be outdone by other kings. However, if a person insists on doing things the enemy's way, Jesus will allow their king to provide for them. Jesus said:

Mt 6:24 No man can serve two masters: for either he will hate the one, and love the other; or else he will hold to the one, and despise the other. Ye cannot serve God and mammon.

If we are the subjects of Jesus Christ, then we will subject ourselves to him and will reap the benefits of His kingdom. Please note that the above sentence is for those who are well established in the Grace and Mercy of God already; it is for those who are at the developmental stage in Christ.

A NOTE ON PROSPERITY

If you think I am speaking only of money then you are missing my point. There are many worldly people with plenty of money who are desperate for the good news of Jesus Christ. They are looking for the person who is healthy, joyous in Christ and prosperous to show them what true Godliness looks like. They are looking for someone like them who has the strength of Christ to abstain from all the sinful options that comes with having a huge sum of money. But they want to see the spiritual side as well as the key that empowers them to live Holy. Let's face it, people who have little money have fewer options for sin.

One of the lessons Christ teaches us is how to abstain from evil when we have the strength, power and resources to commit sin. Avoiding sin that you cannot reach, because of your lack of strength, power or resources, requires no discipline and restraint at all.

1.18

God Wants To Use Your Talents

God gave you your talents before you knew you had them. Now that you are part of the body of Christ, He wants you to give them back to Him to better serve Him.

Ro 11:29 For the gifts and calling of God [are] without repentance.

This scripture simply points out that God has given you your talents, gifts and abilities. He will not decide for you what you should do with them; because He does not micro-manage. It is your choice to use them as you see fit. However, when you give them back to the Lord for His use, you posture yourself to receive a greater blessing.

MY TESTAMONY

When I was sixteen, my grandfather taught me how to play the guitar. He gave me my first guitar and I loved it. Six years later, I was playing guitar every day for at least an hour. I would play when I was sad, happy and lonely. It was my outlet. When I gave my heart to Jesus, I put down the guitar for fear of losing what I had found in Jesus. Several months had passed before I learned that Jesus didn't want me to put down the gift He gave me, He wanted to use my gift for His glory. I'll admit that I was very excited to give back to Him something that I enjoyed doing.

Maybe you have a gift or talent that you love doing but do not know what to do with it now that you have given your heart to Jesus. If so, all you need to do is go to your pastor and share with him your gift, talent or hobby. Ask him if there is room for you to use it for the glory of God.

Some talents need to be cultivated in the things of God before they are suitable to give back to Him. So trust your pastor and believe Jesus will help you get there. Then bask in the glory as you give it back to Him. What a powerful experience!

If your talent is to be used for His glory, then you must realize that He will want you to share it with the body of Christ and/or the lost eventually. After all, His agenda is to save the lost and help develop the saved; any gift and talent that is submissive to His goal will play a part in this. He does not give us these abilities to showcase how wonderful we are; rather to bring others into His presence. This is why cultivating your gift in the house of God under a mentoring pastor is so important. In the house of God, you should be able to practice using your skill for the Lord and make mistakes without destroying your effectiveness. It is being active in the community of the church that your spiritual growth will advance the most. You must learn to minister to others and work with others of like faith. This teaches you to understand the grace of God better. If you do not have a church that you attend regularly, then you are missing a vital element to your blessing and spiritual growth.

Realizing that we all have a gift to offer back to Jesus is the first step. The next steps are:

1. Speak to your pastor about your gift or talent
2. Ask him to direct you in submitting it to the Lord.
3. Join an auxiliary that uses your gift.
4. Practice learning how to use your gift in a Godly way. Many times we use our gift unskillfully, which usually

causes more harm than good, until we learn how to use it more gracefully.

WHAT IF I DON'T KNOW WHAT MY GIFT IS?

That is a great question. My recommendation is that you do what I did; speak with the pastor. If he doesn't have a particular leading for you, suggest to him that you begin working in the auxiliaries, one at a time, for a couple of months each. This exposure to the different ministries in the church will not only help you find your gift, but it will help you be more aware of the other facets of the church.

Once you have experienced all the auxiliaries, you can now choose the one that you enjoyed the most. You see, God gives you the grace to enjoy doing your gift. It will not seem laborious to you.

I must have worked in seven different auxiliaries before I knew what I was called to do. But the good thing is that all my experience in the other auxiliaries has benefitted me tremendously to this day.

Remember this about working in an auxiliary; you must have a regularly scheduled time that you rest from working in the auxiliary so that you can be ministered to. You are no good to God burnt out because of the apparent need. Trust me when I tell you that your regularly scheduled breaks will give you more effectiveness than you can imagine. In addition, God will cover for you when you are being recharged. It is His ministry, not yours. He knows you need rest.

2

WITNESSING

As stated earlier, we have been given the ministry of reconciliation. That means helping others reconcile themselves with God. **Please remember that people do not care about what you know, they want to know how much you care.** Pray that God will put love in your heart for people so that when you witness to them they can sense that you care. Remember, if Jesus can save us, he can save others.

About now, some of you may be thinking that you can't tell people about Jesus because you are not worthy. That is a legalistic (Law) mentality that wants to give strength back to your sin. The only way to defeat it is to say **"His Grace is sufficient for me!"** and go tell someone what Jesus has done for you, and that He will do the same for them.

There was a woman of Samaria mentioned in John the fourth chapter who was truly a sinner. After speaking with Jesus, she went into the city and told all men about Christ. Her qualifications to tell others about Christ boiled down to one single fact; she had an encounter with Jesus. That is the only qualification you need.

Another reason to witness is to give you an advantage over your thoughts. You are in a battle to win the ground of your thought life. Most spiritual battles are found in your thoughts. In order to get the victory, God gave us a principle to follow.

Prov 16:3 ¶ Commit thy works unto the LORD, and thy thoughts shall be established.

Here the Hebrew word for Works is מעשה ma'aseh (pronounced mah-as-eh') meaning: work, needlework, acts, labor, doing, art, deed, a thing done, business, pursuit, undertaking, enterprise, achievement, a thing made, and product. So you can see that as we go out and witness or do anything else for the Lord, it establishes our thoughts.

Below is a script that is very successful for witnessing. It was shared to me by a real man and woman of God; Neal and Marlene Cassata who have given me permission to use it and to allow others to use. They are seasoned evangelists who have started many churches in the outback of Australia. If you would like to ask Jesus in your heart, rededicate your life or use this script to witness, feel free to print this out and use it for yourself or for your soul winning team.

After learning to apply the following script, you will begin to see the effectiveness of not letting others misdirect the conversation. Many responses from people are off handed because of the enemies attempt to place ambiguity around the scriptural requirements for salvation. Just stick to the script. After you have become proficient at using the script with success, feel free to vary your approach to the situation. From time to time you will want to revert back to the script for consistency.

~ Salvation Script ~

1. Has anyone ever told you that God loves you and that He has a wonderful plan for your life?

2. I have a real quick, but important question to ask you. God forbid, but if you were to die this second, do you know for sure, beyond a shadow of a doubt, that you would go to Heaven?

> ~ If they say "Yes", reply "Great, why do you say yes?"

>> ~ If they say "I have Jesus in my heart" or something similar to that, ask them:

>>> ~ With 10 being the greatest and 1 being the least, what number would you give your relationship with Christ?

>>> ~ I want to pray for you: Lord, bless (NAME) to be able to achieve a 10 in his/her relationship with you. I thank you that you will move those hindrances out of the way. In Jesus' Name Amen.

>>> ~ Fill out the Commitment Card. Thank them for their time and move on.

> ~ If they say anything else, (PROCEED WITH SCRIPT Step 3) or "No" or "I hope so" (PROCEED WITH SCRIPT Step 3).

3. Let me quickly share with you what the Holy Bible reads. It reads *"for all have sinned and come short of the glory of God"* and *"for the wages of sin is death, but*

the gift of God is eternal life through Jesus Christ our Lord". The Bible also reads, *"For whosoever shall call upon the name of the Lord shall be saved".* Wouldn't you say that you and I are a "whosoever? Of course you are; all of us are.

4. I'm going to say a quick prayer for you:

> Lord, bless (NAME) and his/her family with long and healthy lives. Jesus, make yourself real to his/her heart. If (NAME) has not received Jesus as his/her Lord and Savior, I pray he/she will do so now.

5. (NAME), if you would like to receive the gift God has for you today, say this after me with your heart and lips out loud.

> Dear Lord Jesus, come into my heart, forgive me of my sin. Wash me and cleanse me. Set me Free. Jesus, thank You that You died for me. I believe that You are risen from the dead, and that You are coming back again for me. Fill me with Your Holy Spirit. Give me a passion for the lost, a hunger for the things of God, and a holy boldness, to preach the gospel of Jesus Christ. I'm Saved: I'm born again, I'm forgiven, and I'm on my way to Heaven, because I have Jesus in my heart!

6. As a minister of reconciliation to God, I tell you today that all of your sins are forgiven. Always remember to run to God and not from Him because He loves you and has a great plan for your life. ~ Welcome to the family of God!

3

LEARNING HOW TO LEARN

Jesus had twelve disciples. During Jesus' three and a half year ministry, these twelve learned of Jesus more intimately than the rest. They walked with Him, ate with Him, slept with Him and ministered to others with Him. This is the relationship Jesus wants with all of us. Now that He is no longer restricted to a mortal body, He can have this close, personal relationship with each individual on the earth at the same time. He is God after all!

The Greek definition for Disciple is μαθητης mathetes (pronounced math-ay-tes') which means: a learner, pupil. The Merriam-Webster's 11th Collegiate Dictionary gives the synonym of disciple as follower. When we accept Jesus into our heart we become a follower of Jesus Christ. Additionally, the word discipline is defined as orderly or prescribed conduct or pattern of behavior. So our place with Christ is to be a follower, pupil, and learner of how to discipline our conduct; pattern our behavior like Him.

As in all educational disciplines, we must be introduced to principles and methodologies that best help us to grasp a greater understanding of the subject matter. Learning how to grow in Jesus Christ is vital for our success with Him. We must learn of Him His way.

In this chapter, we will explore two very powerful principles that not only give you focus on how to cultivate a growing relationship with Christ, but also reveal to you how God teaches us in his word and revelation.

Here we will look at Jesus' command to learn of Him. We will also look at how God opens His word to us. Finally, we will look at the pattern set for the followers and leaders.

3.1

Come Unto Me

Matt 11:28 Come unto me, all [ye] that labour and are heavy laden, and I will give you rest. **29** Take my yoke upon you, and learn of me; for I am meek and lowly in heart: and ye shall find rest unto your souls. **30** For my yoke [is] easy, and my burden is light.

When most of us take on a new subject, we prefer to learn it our way. Truth is, you are probably going to learn it best your way. However, when it comes to learning about your Savior, Jesus Christ, it is best that you learn of Him His way. Jesus Christ not only knows how to teach us, he knows how we best learn. After all, he is the manufacture of mankind. He knows us better than we know ourselves.

Jesus is giving us a directive with the results in Matthew 11:28 – 30. Let's look at it as a list:

- Come unto Jesus ~ He will give you Rest
- Take Jesus' yoke and learn of Him ~ You will find Rest in your souls
- His yoke is easy and His burden is light

The statement "Come unto me" is an imperative tense. That means that it is vital that we come to Jesus if we want Him to give us rest. Additionally, if we take His yoke and learn of Him, we will find rest in our soul. Then He reassures us that it is easier than we think by telling us that His yoke is easy and His burden is light.

I'd like to point out here that there are two different kinds of "Rest" mentioned here; Jesus did not repeat himself.

The first Rest comes from the Greek word αναπαυω anapauo (pronounced an-ap-ow'-o); meaning:

❖ to cause or permit one to cease from any movement or labor in order to recover and collect his strength
❖ to give rest, refresh, to give one's self rest, take rest
❖ to keep quiet, of calm and patient expectation

Here is the part that excites me, anapauo comes from the root word παυω pauo (pronounced pow'-o); meaning

• to make to cease or desist
• to restrain a thing or person from something
• to cease, to leave off
• have got release from sin
• no longer stirred by its incitements and seductions

As we come to Jesus, he restrains the influence of sin on our lives and gives us rest from the struggle. All we have to do is run to Jesus when we are battling an urge to do something sinful; He restrains it for us. Praise the Lord! This is why:

Rom 10:13 For whosoever shall call upon the name of the Lord shall be saved.

The second Rest in Matthew 28: 29 comes from the Greek word αναπαυσις anapausis (pronounced an-ap'-ow-sis) which has a different meaning of:

1) intermission, cessation of any motion, business or labour
2) rest, recreation

Not only does Jesus give us relief from the pressures of sin, he gives us rest from our labors and gives us the ability to enjoy recreation. God knows that when we balance our life with recreation we are able to be more productive. Remember that the scriptures share that laughter has a season.

Ecclesiastes (Ecc) 3: 4 A time to weep, and **a time to laugh**; a time to mourn, and a time to dance; …

Returning to Matt 11:28-30, Soul in verse 29 is the Greek word ψυχη psuche (pronounced soo-khay'); meaning:

- the breath of life
- the vital force which animates the body and shows itself in breathing
- the seat of the feelings, desires, affections, aversions (our heart, soul etc.)
- the (human) soul in so far as it is constituted that by the right use of the aids offered it by God it can attain its highest end and secure eternal blessedness, the soul regarded as a moral being designed for everlasting life
- the soul as an essence which differs from the body and is not dissolved by death (distinguished from other parts of the body)

This is the rest that soothes the soul and calms the spirit. If you are struggling with emotions, desires, affections or find yourself conflicted, this is the rest that you need. So let's take His yoke and learn more of Him so we can get both kinds of rest!

Learning of Jesus and taking His yoke upon you go hand in hand. Let's look at how Jesus teaches us.

3.2

Here A Little, There A Little

The bible is not written like a regular book in that it is not linear. Reading it from beginning to end (Genesis to Revelations) will not bring you to understand the first principles of God quicker. In fact, it may cause you to lose interest in reading the bible and then never reach the first principles. You see, the Old Testament is a picture of Jesus Christ concealed and the New Testament is a picture of Jesus Christ revealed. It's not that we won't understand some of the stories in the Old Testament; it's just that in order to get a revelation of Jesus in the Old Testament, we need to be familiar with Him in the New Testament first; a luxury that the Old Testament saints didn't have.

God knew that our first inclination would be to read the Bible from beginning to end so He gave us a scripture to inform us of the various ways He will teach us and help us grow.

Isa 28:9 ¶ Whom shall he teach knowledge? and whom shall he make to understand doctrine? [them that are] weaned from the milk, [and] drawn from the breasts. **10** For precept [must be] upon precept, precept upon precept; line upon line, line upon line; here a little, [and] there a little:

Let's look at this scripture a little closer:

1. Knowledge and understanding doctrine comes to those who are weaned from milk.

   Like a birth of a child, this implies a birthing stage, a suckling stage, a weaning stage and a maturing stage. When we first get saved, we are born again. We must learn of the basic principles of God from the milk of the word (simple concepts). After a period of growth, we mature enough to add to our foundation and begin to take in stronger concepts of the word. At this point we begin our maturing stage.

The purpose of this book is to bring you from a birthing stage to a maturing stage.

2. Precepts will be presented and then built upon with other precepts.

Just like an arm, when we are small we don't cut our arm off to grow a bigger one; we add to what has already been established. This is a precept in itself. We grow in Christ by adding to what He has already given us through learning of Him through the Word of God.

The Hebrew word for precept is צו tsav (pronounced tsawv); meaning commandment or ordinance.

For example: Jesus gave a new precept when He said:

Matt 5:43 ¶ Ye have heard that it hath been said, Thou shalt love thy neighbour, and hate thine enemy. **44** But I say unto you, Love your enemies, bless them that curse you, do good to them that hate you, and pray for them which despitefully use you, and persecute you; **45** That ye may be the children of your Father which is in heaven: for he maketh his sun to rise on the evil and on the good, and sendeth rain on the just and on the unjust. **46** For if ye love them which love you, what reward have ye? do not even the publicans the same? **47** And if ye salute your brethren only, what do ye more [than others]? do not even the publicans so?

This was a direct commandment of what Jesus expects from Christians. You see love is a choice; not a feeling.

This precept commands us to love our enemies.

3. Line upon line in the word of God.

    God does not rule out the necessity of reading His Word and understanding it in context. He just places precepts ahead of linear reading of His Word to quicken our ability to reach the maturing stage.

    God is multidimensional, He has layer upon layer of revelation in His word. Line upon line is a way to reveal one layer.

    It is not a bad idea if your daily reading included a chapter in the bible a day. Start reading in the New Testament until you have read it several times before you begin in Genesis.

4. Here a little and there a little.

    Many revelations of Jesus Christ come from seeing a scripture from the Old Testament connect to another from the New Testament or from one book to another (The bible has 66 books within it).

    For example:

    - Jesus' birth was prophesied by the prophet Isaiah

Isa 9:6 For unto us a child is born, unto us a son is given: and the government shall be upon his shoulder: and his name shall be called Wonderful, Counsellor, The mighty God, The everlasting Father, The Prince of Peace.

- Isaiah also prophesied that Jesus' birth would be by a virgin.

  Isa 7:14 Therefore the Lord himself shall give you a sign; Behold, a virgin shall conceive, and bear a son, and shall call his name Immanuel.

- The location of Jesus' birth was prophesied by the prophet Micah

  Mic 5:2 But thou, Bethlehem Ephratah, [though] thou be little among the thousands of Judah, [yet] out of thee shall he come forth unto me [that is] to be ruler in Israel; whose goings forth [have been] from of old, from everlasting.

This is an example of "Here a little and There a little". God has many wonderful revelations waiting for you; if you let the Holy Ghost lead you through the scriptures, He will connect the scriptures together for you. For now, it is good to let experienced men and women of God show you what the Lord has showed them so that you can see the various ways Jesus opens up to us.

As a moment of encouragement, when you read the account of Jesus' birth in the New Testament, you should get the revelation that God had this all planned out. All the drama, moving parts and circumstances were used by God to fulfill what he had promised.

Now you can look at your life and consider that He is doing the same for you in the middle of your circumstances and all your moving parts. Know that your destination is victorious through Jesus Christ! He has it all planned out for you!

Rom 8:28 And we know that all things work together for good to them that love God, to them who are the called according to [his] purpose.

Jer 29:11 For I know the thoughts that I think toward you, saith the LORD, thoughts of peace, and not of evil, to give you an expected end.

Jesus is saying that He's got you!

Hallelujah!

This type of "Here a little and there a little" can build your confidence and faith in Jesus Christ like no other. Let us dive into the waters of the word and search out the depths of His revelations.

In order to understand the deeper things, we must first understand the shallower things.

3.3

Show, Teach, Then Do

When Jesus was teaching the disciples how to baptize, He demonstrated, taught and then He had them baptize others under His supervision before they were to go out on their own. How do I know this? Let's look at some scriptures.

Jesus Baptized: (Show)

John 3:22 ¶ After these things came Jesus and his disciples into the land of Judaea; and there he tarried with them, and baptized.

Jesus Teaches the Disciples How to Baptize: (Teach)

John 4:1 ¶ When therefore the Lord knew how the Pharisees had heard that Jesus made and baptized more disciples than John, **2** (Though Jesus himself baptized not, but his disciples,)

Paul Baptizes: (Do)

Ac 19:4 Then said Paul, John verily baptized with the baptism of repentance, saying unto the people, that they should believe on him which should come after him, that is, on Christ Jesus. **5** When they heard [this], they were baptized in the name of the Lord Jesus.

Incidentally, Paul was taught by the other disciples how to baptize; not Jesus. It is safe to say that they taught him the same way they were taught.

Another example of Show, Teach Then Do occurred when Jesus washed the disciple's feet after their last supper together:

John 13:4 He riseth from supper, and laid aside his garments; and took a towel, and girded himself. **5** After that he poureth water into a bason, and began to wash the disciples' feet, and to wipe them with the towel wherewith he was girded. **6** Then cometh he to Simon Peter: and Peter saith unto him, Lord, dost thou wash my feet? **7** Jesus answered and said unto him, What I do thou knowest not now; but thou shalt know hereafter. **8** Peter saith unto him, Thou shalt never wash my feet. Jesus answered him, If I wash thee not, thou hast no part with me. **9** Simon Peter saith unto him, Lord, not my feet only, but also my hands and my head. **10** Jesus saith to him, He that is washed needeth not save to wash his feet, but is clean every whit: and ye are clean, but not all. **11** For he knew who should betray him; therefore said he, Ye are not all clean. **12** So after he had washed their feet, and had taken his garments, and was set down again, he said unto them, Know ye what I have done to you? **13** Ye call me Master and Lord: and ye say well; for so I am. **14** If I then, your Lord and Master, have washed your feet; ye also ought to wash one another's feet. **15** For I have given you an example, that ye should do as I have done to you. **16** Verily, verily, I say unto you, The servant is not greater than his lord; neither he that is sent greater than he that sent him. **17** If ye know these things, **happy are ye if ye do them**.

We can find happiness by doing what Jesus tells us to do! This is why it is so important for leaders to lead by example; others are watching to see what behavior is acceptable. What they see, they will copy. As a follower, we need to know the word of God to ensure that our behavior is pleasing to the Lord; even when leadership has failed to lead by example.

4

From Thought to Deed

Our actions are a result of our thoughts. Our thought life is a result of what we meditate on. What do we spend our time thinking about? Jesus dealt with the thought life of mankind many times:

Matt 9:4 And Jesus knowing their thoughts said, Wherefore think ye evil in your hearts?

Matt 5:28 But I say unto you, That whosoever looketh on a woman to lust after her hath committed adultery with her already in his heart.

On the Day of Judgment, our thoughts, motives, hidden agendas, will and deeds will be revealed. If we don't judge ourselves here on earth, we will surely face judgment in heaven. We must deal with every one of our character flaws as the Lord brings them to our attention. Many times, we don't like what we see and are tempted to sweep them under the rug or pretend that we didn't see it. With the help of Jesus, we can overcome our weaknesses and be found blameless before God on the Day of Judgment.

Our thoughts strive to manifest as self-fulfilling prophecies. We stop them when we speak out with our voice, even in a whisper, Jesus' name. Sometimes your surroundings are such that you can speak out a scripture.

Prov 23: 6 ¶ Eat thou not the bread of him that hath an evil eye, neither desire thou his dainty meats: **7** For as he thinketh in his heart, so is he: Eat and drink, saith he to thee; but his heart is not with thee. **8** The morsel which thou hast eaten shalt thou vomit up, and lose thy sweet words.

Proverbs 23:6 & 7 reveals that an evil eye, or a person who continually looks towards evil, does so because their thoughts are continually on evil so they become evil in God's eyes. This principle would also apply to those who continually strive to think on the things of God. They become righteous in God's eyes.

WHICH THOUGHT IS MINE?

The battle is in the mind, the thought life. Not all thoughts we have are ours. Some thoughts are from spirits, principalities and the devil. The biggest trick he uses is to get us to claim those filthy thoughts as our own. Once we speak those thoughts with our voice, they become our thoughts. Do not speak with voice or whisper ungodly thoughts. In order to change the direction of your thoughts all you have to do is speak out loud or in a whisper something else. If you call on Jesus, he will bring your thoughts back into righteousness.

Don't give up! Even if you have to call on His name, Jesus, moment by moment, do it! This is a struggle to take control of your mind. Speak the word of God.

As we develop our ability to think on things good, righteous, and Godly, we will begin to behave in a Godly manner.

Notice that our heart is closely connected to our thoughts. Additionally, what's in our heart comes out of our mouth.

Luke 6:45 A good man out of the good treasure of his heart bringeth forth that which is good; and an evil man out of the evil treasure of his heart bringeth forth that which is evil: for of the abundance of the heart his mouth speaketh.

We can listen to our words and determine where we are in our spiritual walk.

Some of us curse and must realize that a curse is still in our heart. Until we learn to keep control of the reigns of our thoughts, we will never get the victory over our words and completely enter in to what God has for us.

Some of us don't curse any longer (Praise the Lord for your Development!) but say things that are contrary to the word of God. Anything contrary to the word of God is against God and can be considered Anti-God or Anti-Christ. This is how the enemy sneaks into a Christian's life and slowly but surely chokes it to death! We as Christians, give up our right to disagree with the word of God. This is why we must work at not contradicting the word of God in our thoughts, words and deeds.

Prov 4:23 Keep thy heart with all diligence; for out of it [are] the issues of life.

We must guard our heart diligently to keep the enemy from swallowing up our life that was given to us by way of the cross.

Jesus receives a better witness when a Christian is living the LIFE they have been given privilege to enjoy. We receive increased life as we increase our abilities to control and discipline our thoughts. Here are some guidelines on how to work on our spiritual growth at the battlefront of the thoughts. WHAT SHOULD I BE THINKING ABOUT?

Php 4:8 Finally, brethren, whatsoever things are true, whatsoever things are honest, whatsoever things are just, whatsoever things are pure, whatsoever things are lovely, whatsoever things are of good report; if there be any virtue, and if there be any praise, think on these things.

Philippians above gives us a standard to measure our thought life according to the Word of God. Anything else is sin. I am not implying that we should be thinking on the bible continually. It is honest and just for us to think about pleasing our spouses, children, family, friends and employer in a Godly way. We should think about how to be a better boss, employee, vender and even customer. We should think about how to serve better in our local church and how to beautify our lives in our homes. God is a God of the Living not the dead! So Live!

When we find our thoughts deviating from those mentioned in Philippians 4:8, we must take action!

2 Cor 10: 3 For though we walk in the flesh, we do not war after the flesh: **4** (For the weapons of our warfare are not carnal, but mighty through God to the pulling down of strong holds;) **5 Casting down imaginations**, and every high thing that exalteth itself against the knowledge of God, and **bringing into captivity every thought to the obedience of Christ;**

When I have a battle in my mind, sometimes I quote 2nd Corinthians (2 Cor) 10:3-5 and this brings my thoughts into the obedience of Christ. Sometimes I speak out Jesus' name to bring my thoughts back in obedience. Both of these techniques work.

Jesus has given us power over our thought life and we must cast down our thoughts and imaginations that are contrary to the word of God. These strongholds in our minds can be cast down!

When you find yourself struggling with a thought, speak Jesus' name as many times as you need from your mouth. Even in a whisper, that name above all names will cause your thoughts to be freed from that bondage. Sometimes the battle rages furiously and we find we ourselves pleading the blood on our thoughts moment by moment. You can take this new ground if you refuse to relent! Take it by Force!

Matt 11:12 And from the days of John the Baptist until now the kingdom of heaven suffereth violence, and the violent take it by force.

OUR ACTIONS (DEEDS)

We can do nothing without thinking it first.

Eph 6:5 Servants, be obedient to them that are your masters according to the flesh, with fear and trembling, in singleness of your heart, as unto Christ; **6** Not with eyeservice, as menpleasers; but as the servants of Christ, doing the will of God from the heart; **7** With good will doing service, as to the Lord, and not to men: **8** Knowing that whatsoever good thing any man doeth, the same shall he receive of the Lord, whether he be bond or free. **9** And, ye masters, do the same things unto them, forbearing threatening: knowing that your Master also is in heaven; neither is there respect of persons with him. **10** ¶ Finally, my brethren, be strong in the Lord, and in the power of his might.

Show me an employee or boss who is aware of and strives to keep the scripture above and I will show you a productive and successful person.

The way to judge the things in your heart is to be honest with yourself and God. Observe what is in your thought life. Observe your actions and the words from your mouth. This is why speaking out scriptures is so powerful; it helps you bring your thought life back into Christ.

Matt 12:34 O generation of vipers, how can ye, being evil, speak good things? For out of the abundance of the heart the mouth speaketh.

If you have sinned, ask for forgiveness and work on not continuing in the sin. This is where Ephesians 6:10 was meant to be applied. In some things, we will need the power of his might to overcome them in our lives. You can win this battle as long as you study your thoughts. Truly we move from our thoughts to our deeds.

God has already provided you the victory. All you need to do is apply these principles and you will succeed if you don't give up.

The development of a Christian is cyclic. Meaning, there are seasons of continual battle and seasons of rest. Don't be alarmed if you find yourself calling on Jesus' name moment by moment and later, not as often. This is the normal cycle of our development; to go from one season to another. This process also implies that it is common to go from rest to continually calling on Jesus' name. Every step you grow will seem like you are repeating a challenge but you aren't! Its just like climbing a ladder; every rung looks the same and the effort to climb is the same. The truth is... you're getting higher!

5

ANOTHER BLESSING FOR YOU

There is a thing called out in the bible as the "Commanded Blessing". Where is this blessing? How can we obtain it?

Ps 133:1 ¶ <<A Song of degrees of David.>> Behold, how good and how pleasant it is for brethren to dwell together in unity! **2** It is like the precious ointment upon the head, that ran down upon the beard, even Aaron's beard: that went down to the skirts of his garments; **3** As the dew of Hermon, and as the dew that descended upon the mountains of Zion: for there the LORD commanded the blessing, even life for evermore.

Verse 3 point out two benefits: The Lord's commanded blessing and life for evermore. This specific blessing and life comes with Christians dwelling together in unity.

Many people believe that they don't have to go to church to have a relationship with Jesus and they are correct. However, it is an immature Christian that lacks understanding in the word of God who subscribes to this mentality. Another blessing, one that is commanded by God comes when we connect to a body of believers of Jesus Christ. Belonging to a local ministry is vital for one to receive the Lord's commanded blessing. This commanded blessing is found in the assembly of Christians. This is not dependant on man; rather it is promised and commanded by God.

You may say that you are fine not going to church. The truth is, you are missing a vital part from the Lord's provisions. If you have been away for some time, you may no longer remember the blessings you received being among a fellowship.

We need all the life we can get from God, Jesus and the Holy Ghost. There is a portion of life that comes with being in corporate worship. Some may call it synergetic, but I call it Jesus dwelling in the middle of His people.

Mt 18:20 For where two or three are gathered together in my name, there am I in the midst of them.

Some things require that we come together to see the results of our prayer come to pass.

Mt 18:19 Again I say unto you, That if two of you shall agree on earth as touching any thing that they shall ask, it shall be done for them of my Father which is in heaven.

In order to reach a deeper depth with Christ, which translates to a greater amount of blessing, privileges, and favor with God, we must commit to the instructions and directions given in the word of God. In Hebrews 10:25, God uses Paul to admonish us not to forsake assembling ourselves because he wants us to receive the Lord's commanded blessing.

Heb 10: 23 Let us hold fast the profession of our faith without wavering; (for he is faithful that promised;) **24** And let us consider one another to provoke unto love and to good works: **25** Not forsaking the assembling of ourselves together, as the manner of some is; but exhorting one another: and so much the more, as ye see the day approaching.

When we make excuses or avoid going to church, we forfeit the commanded blessing for that service. Personally, I can't afford to miss any blessings that I might need to make it through the next week!

Many saints are unaware that the Lord commanded the blessing to be in brothers and sisters dwelling together in unity. Where do brothers and sisters come together that they can be in unity? Simply it's during worship services, bible studies, prayer night, and Sunday school.

The blessing cannot be obtained with a gathering without unity. When men are competing against each other in the church for positions and power, there is no unity. When women are comparing themselves against each other instead of loving the unique qualities of one another, there is no unity and the commanded blessing is missing.

To provoke a commanded blessing to be set before us, we must get connected to a person who follows the Lord. Stop competing, comparing, and worrying what others will think and start focusing on what Jesus thinks.

FRICTION IN THE CHURCH

When two or more people try to do anything on this earth together, there will be disagreement at some point. Please know that the disagreement is a way of helping us mature. We must know that we can disagree respectfully and if no resolution comes forward, we can agree to disagree. My pastor will always have the final say in our disagreements. He knows that I will voice my concern and he is counting on it. He also knows that I will back him up on his final decision. This means that I will not speak to anyone else about my disagreement. If I still feel strongly about it, I will commit it to the hands of the Lord in prayer.

If I disagree with a person in church and they do not have spiritual authority over me. I do what my pastor does; I listen to see if God is trying to lead in a specific way. I thank them for bringing up their concern and promise to take it to the Lord in prayer. If it needs to be solved immediately, I choose the best advice over my own. It is not about me, it is about Jesus.

GETTING IN AGREEMENT

Finally, we must get in agreement with the man or woman of God established as our spiritual head-ship. We accomplish this by supporting the local ministry with our life. Bishop Holcomb, a great man of God, defines it this way "life is our time, talents, possessions and money." We spend our life working with these attributes. Jesus wants us to give our life to him and one way we do this is by being active in a church, giving a portion of our time, talents, possessions and money to support the local ministry.

Matt 18:19 Again I say unto you, That if two of you shall agree on earth as touching anything that they shall ask, it shall be done for them of my Father which is in heaven.

Going to church puts us in an environment of saints who are willing to touch in agreement with us to get the results that we need. If you can't see yourself getting anyone to touch and agree with you in prayer, try your pastor or minster. As you can see, this is in place for you to succeed.

Jude 7:2 And the LORD said unto Gideon, The people that are with thee are too many for me to give the Midianites into their hands, lest Israel vaunt themselves against me, saying, Mine own hand hath saved me.

Gideon wasn't dwelling in unity with those who were with him until he had 300 remaining. Unity doesn't equate with large numbers but always with hearts with the same vision and faith.

1Sam 13:22 So it came to pass in the day of battle, that there was neither sword nor spear found in the hand of any of the people that were with Saul and Jonathan: but with Saul and with Jonathan his son was there found. **23** And the garrison of the Philistines went out to the passage of Michmash.

1Sam 14: 6 And Jonathan said to the young man that bare his armour, Come, and let us go over unto the garrison of these uncircumcised: it may be that the LORD will work for us: for there is no restraint to the LORD to save by many or by few. **7** And his armourbearer said unto him, Do all that is in thine heart: turn thee; behold, I am with thee according to thy heart.

1Sa 14:12 And the men of the garrison answered Jonathan and his armourbearer, and said, Come up to us, and we will shew you a thing. And Jonathan said unto his armourbearer, Come up after me: for the LORD hath delivered them into the hand of Israel. **13** And Jonathan climbed up upon his hands and upon his feet, and his armourbearer after him: and they fell before Jonathan; and his armourbearer slew after him.

Jonathan and his armor bearer performed a great victory due to their ability to walk in agreement in heart, vision, and faith.

Don't miss the Lord's commanded blessing by not gathering with saints of like precious faith. The very results that we seek could be waiting on us to operate this principle for the release.

Remember, it is not surprising to find sick people in a hospital. So finding people who are working on their character, integrity, friendliness, smiling, and greetings in a church should not surprise you either. We all need improvement, so be patient; God is not finished with us yet.

6

WHAT'S NEXT?

After reading this book, hopefully a lot of pressure has been relieved about your new walk with Jesus. God has invested a great amount of effort to have a relationship with you. He ensured that it would be easy for you to receive His son and be one of His disciples. The journey with Jesus is exciting and rewarding.

Now you may be asking "Where do I go from here?" I invite you to read the next chapter (More of My Personal Testimonies). It is my prayer that it will encourage your heart on how great Jesus really is. Remember, if He did it for me, He will do it for you.

Next, I recommend my book "Second Things Second". This book is the natural follow on to this book. It will root you and ground you in what Hebrews 6:1~2 states as the "Doctrine of Christ".

Heb 6:1 ¶ Therefore leaving the principles of the **doctrine of Christ**, let us go on unto perfection; not laying again the foundation of repentance from dead works, and of faith toward God, **2** Of the doctrine of baptisms, and of laying on of hands, and of resurrection of the dead, and of eternal judgment.

This scripture identifies a foundation that consists of six pillars. They are:

- Repentance From Dead Works
- Faith Toward God
- The Doctrine Of Baptisms
- Laying On Of Hands
- Resurrection Of The Dead
- Eternal Judgment

Every Christian should be familiar with the scriptures that pertain to these six subjects known as the Doctrine of Christ. Second Things Second is a great way to be introduced or refreshed on them.

7

MORE OF MY PERSONAL TESTAMONIES

I hope that this chapter encourages you to keep on keeping on in Christ. I want you to know that Jesus is real and if he will interact with me in the natural, He will do the same for you. Be Blessed!

In Germany, Pastor McMillan asked me to pastor a church for a Pastor who needed to go back to the states for a month. I was horrified and honored. During this time I was given a bird's eye view of what it takes to be a pastor. I was required to put a large amount of effort into this task. Being led by the Holy Ghost for me personally is not like being led for a church; although there are some similarities. My dependency on Jesus grew as I was required to bring the word every service. Praise the Lord that the church was returned to the Pastor in the same condition he left it.

My lesson learned is that no matter how much I know about the word of God, I will need Jesus to direct my steps to give a relevant word to the people.

~

Going back to my beginning with Christ; there I was, in the church, enjoying a personal relationship with Jesus, wanting nothing when, one Sunday, a visiting family came to sing at our church. They were called the Family Circle. A mother and six daughters sang and the presence of God filled the church wonderfully. I had never heard such music in my life. I particularly noticed one of the daughters who seemed to stand out more than the rest. I did not think any more of it after that night. However, I began to see her face as I prayed in the mornings. I'd like to tell you that I knew that the Lord was presenting her as my future wife but the truth is I thought that I was lusting. Then I thought I was being attacked by the devil during my prayer time so I rebuked that foul spirit. It's funny now, but then I was afraid that I may be losing what I had so desperately tried to maintain; a strong relationship with God. I admitted that she was beautiful to my pastor and he raised an eyebrow at me; he had never done that before. Did I forget to tell you that my pastor operated in the prophetic at times? Without getting into too much detail, in order for me to court Georgette, I would need to sell my motorcycle, buy a car and return from a deployment in Europe. Ironically, that is exactly what happened in the space of one month. So with the obstacles removed, I called her and asked if she would like to go out. We dated for six months and were engaged for six months.

My lesson learned was "Mt 6:33 But seek ye first the kingdom of God, and his righteousness; and all these things shall be added unto you."

~

Remember that I needed to sell my motorcycle and buy a car in order to court my wife? I was an airman in the Air Force and not making much money. My only form of transportation was a motorcycle that I had just paid off. I didn't have the funds to purchase a car. At the time, my wife and I were in a church that didn't believe women should wear pants. So it was impractical for me to take her on a date with a motorcycle. She lived in a small town forty minutes away so I just put the thought of courting her to rest. One day, my pastor told me that he saw a car for sale with my name on it. I remember thinking, Lord, if you want me to buy a car, you will have to help me sell my motorcycle.

Not many days later, I was at a stop light about thirteen cars back. I was slowly rolling forward; the light had just turned red. All of a sudden, I was hit from behind by a ninja motorcycle. The impact was so hard that my front wheel hit the bumper of the car in front of me and the frame acted like a pole vault. My rear tire lifted off the ground and catapulted the ninja into a fenced in yard where the driver landed. The Lord ensured that I was not injured but my motorcycle frame was broken. Fortunately, the ninja driver only hurt his leg, which he recovered just fine. Who has ever heard of a motorcycle rear ending another motorcycle?

I had just paid off the motorcycle and the insurance adjuster totaled my bike. For some odd reason, the value of my bike had gone up a thousand dollars. So I used the money to buy the car that my pastor said had my name on it (it was a real nice car). Three days after purchasing the car, I called my wife and asked her out on a date. We courted for six months and were engaged for six months.

My lesson learned here was, I don't have to stress, struggle or strain to make God's will happen for my life. I can just trust that all things are working together for my good.

~

Upon my engagement, I called my parents to inform them. Their response was forbidding and I couldn't believe this was happing. My parents were reacting to my wife without ever meeting her just because she was of another race. In fact, my father said some very harsh words to me of which I could not answer back, because I had just learned about honoring my father and mother. I had also searched the scriptures concerning my decision to marry Georgette. It came down to one important factor; God did not want marriage to separate me from my relationship with Him. Georgette was determined to keep Jesus first in her life so I figured it was truly a match made in heaven (I found out later that we both had secretly prayed that God would stop us if it was not His will). I was devastated that my parents were so adamantly against the marriage. After I was married, my name was not allowed to be mentioned and my parents took my pictures off the wall. I was forced to go to God on this and He said that if I would serve him that he would fix this. I thought it to be a deal in my favor because I was not going to stop serving Jesus over this.

Five years later I visited my Dad and Mother with Georgette and my two children. Since that day, Dad made sure that he hugged Georgette upon arriving and leaving. This is huge because he never liked to show public display of affection.

What I found out later was how God fixed it. My parents had some people move next door to them and they fast became every day friends. My parent's neighbors would brag on their son who was in the military as was I. They also doted on their daughter in-law and how wonderful she was. One day, their son and his wife came home to visit and the parents couldn't wait to introduce them to my parents. They brought their white son and black wife over and introduced them as if there was nothing wrong. Apparently, this caused my parent to reconsider their position. I know that God set that up!

My lesson learned was that God knows my heart and the pain that I have suffered over this and because I would not let go of my faith, he moved on my behalf.

As I write this book, my wife and I have been married for thirty one years.

~

I was working for a well known electronics store and a man came in and bought a computer. He was a big man, sort of intimidating and he could cuss the wall paper off of a wall. While purchasing a computer, he told me that he was going to use the computer to run his rabbit business. Easter was coming up and it was the busiest time of the year for him. He was concerned about getting it up and running correctly. I taught him some things and gave him my personal phone number to call me if he needed any help.

I received several phone calls from this man and at times we spoke for what seemed like hours. I almost regretted giving him my phone number. Finally I told the Lord that I would share with him the gospel if I could get to his house. It wasn't long when he invited me to his house to see his rabbits. I accepted and visited with intentions of telling him about Jesus. While at his house, I saw his business and we sat down in the living room to have some soda and talk. I was overcome with fear and never shared Jesus with him.

One week later his wife came into the store to tell me that he had died of a heart attack. I was horrified and felt like I had failed my Lord. Countless times I was under mental attack over my failure. Then I learned about the true Grace of God and that He died for my past, present and future sins. I wept at this realization and turned to Christ with gratitude for His kindness.

My lesson learned was: His Grace is sufficient for me. I also have resolved in my heart that when I am lead into a situation that needs an ambassador for the Lord, I obey because He has forgiven others past, present and future sins. Jesus took the responsibility to reach all of mankind. GRACE! He already knows. I am still in right standing with Jesus because His work on the cross was a complete work. AMEN!

~

During my being disowned by my parents, a prophet came to me and told me that I would lead my father to the Lord. At the time I didn't see the opportunity so I put that word on the shelf and waited to see it come to pass. My father was stricken with dementia and during one of his episodes of shutting down, my mother called me and I lead dad in the prayer of salvation just in time. He went to the hospital and was released three days later because he was lucid again. I thought that the word of the Lord had been fulfilled. Three months later, I was talking with my dad and asked him "Dad, do you remember when you asked Jesus to come into your heart?" he replied, no. I then said, "Well you did, and did you know that when you get to heaven, there will be a new body for you? No more bad breath, long toe nails or a broken body." Dad thanked me for those kind words. Later that day he became catatonic.

Hospice had come to help with the final days. I came home to be with dad. Three days later, there I was standing to the left of my dad holding his hand, my mom and sisters were gathered around his bed as well. I secretly prayed to Jesus to stir dad if there was anything he needed to do before going. Right then, he turned his head and looked into my eyes with an intense gaze that I could not shake. I was so engulfed in his stare that I forgot about my surroundings and said out loud "Jesus" every time he breathed in. My dad tried to mouth Jesus back when he breathed out. After the second time, he turned his head and breathed his last breath.

The anointing of the Lord Jesus was so strong in the room that I was amazed at the astonished look of all in the room. Later the Hospice person said that she had never witnessed anything so beautiful and when she passes, she wanted me to be there for her. She also said that I had helped my dad pass through to the Lord. I can't help but wonder what would have happened if I had not dealt with my unforgiveness and resentment for the way I was disowned.

My lesson learned was that we have an eternity to live as Christians and it starts once we ask Jesus into our heart. All of the things we go through in this mortal body is to prove that we can live in joy unspeakable regardless. He came to give us abundant life NOW!

I realize that not many have the opportunity to mend things with their families. I want to encourage you to take it to the Lord Jesus Christ and leave it there. Stop holding it against yourself before you hinder your ability to do Jesus' will. His will is that you live with no condemnation.

FINAL THOUGHTS

Remember that Jesus Loves you; so do I.

In His Hands,

Steve

For Him Ministries

REFERENCES

Hebrew and Chaldee Lexicon to the Old Testament, Gesenius and Fürst, Boston: A.I. Bradley & Co.

James Strong, Abingdon's Strong's Exhaustive Concordance of the Bible, New Jersey, 1890 – James Strong, Key Word Comparison 1980 – Abingdon

Software: *Online Bible Edition*, Authorized Version of the King James Bible, Strong's Concordance
Version 2.00.04, June 2006

Thompson Chain Reference Study Bible King James Version, Kirkbride Bible Company, Inc. Indiana, 1988

Works by Pastor Steve Morgan

~ First Things First   (What Every Christian Should Know)

Christianity is really very easy. This book shows you
how scriptures make it so easy. If you are a new
believer or a believer who is returning to your first love,
this is for you. First Things First starts from receiving
Christ into your heart and finishes with some basic
principles to build on a foundation laid by the word of
God. Pastor Steve also shares some personal
testimonies with the principles learned that will help
you avoid some of the challenges he faced as a new
born again believer.

~ Second Things Second   (The Doctrine of Christ)

This book covers the principles of the doctrine of Christ
as mentioned in Hebrews 6:1~2. We will cover the six
pillars mentioned here.

To be perfect you must stay under the grace of God.
To do that you must learn more of His provisions for
you. These can be found in the Doctrine of Christ.
The foundation of the Doctrine of Christ is supported
by six pillars which are:

- Repentance From Dead Works
- Faith Toward God
- The Doctrine Of Baptisms
- Laying On Of Hands
- Resurrection Of The Dead

- Eternal Judgment

Every Christian should be encouraged by Hebrews 6:1~2 to learn of these pillars and build a foundation that cannot be moved.

~ God's Blueprint for Spiritual Growth and Reward
(The Mosaic Tabernacle)

There are many examples of how we are to grow in God's likeness. The Tabernacle, built under the supervision of Moses, is also a map to maturity. Here you will learn some of the depths of God and His commitment to maintaining a relationship with you.

~ The Wife's Secret Weapon

Relationships are very easy but they require special tools you already have. With this book, you will learn about your "Secret Weapon". This "Secret Weapon will empower you to reach your husband emotionally deeper than ever before. You will learn how to get past the WALL that seems to frustrate you when you speak to your spouse. He will actually respond to you like a real human being! Can you imagine him talking to you in more than a few words at a time? This book will show you how to draw this person out. He really is your perfect man! When you have accomplished all the challenges in this book, you will have increased in influence in the marriage by 100 fold. This is the latest information on communicating across gender lines. If you wish that you could get your point across to the opposite sex, this book gives you what you need to succeed while having fun doing it. You won't believe how powerful these tools are until you try them!

~ The Husband's Toolbox

Relationships are really very easy, but they require special tools you already have. With this book, you will learn how to use them to their full benefit. You will also discover why your wife is the way she is and how to work with her as you were designed by God! You will learn how to make sure she never wants to leave your side. After completing the challenges in this book, you will have obtained your rightful position as the Man of your house. This is the latest information on communicating across gender lines. If you wish that you could get your point across to the opposite sex, this book gives you what you need to succeed! You won't believe how powerful these tools are until you try them!

PASTOR STEVE MORGAN's CREDENTIALS

Alumni of Sonship School of the Firstborn
        Bishop Nathaniel Holcomb
        Covenant Connections International (CCI)
        Kaleen, TX

Masters in Business Administration (MBA)
        Troy University
        Troy, AL

Bachelor of Arts in Business Management
        Ashford University
        Clinton, IA

Associates in Applied Science in Human Relations
        Community College of the Air Force (CCAF)

Associates in Applied Science in Electronic
Engineering Technology
        CCAF

Pastor Steve is the founder and president of For Him Ministries. He has performed as a stand-in pastor for several churches in Germany and in Florida; allowing for vacations and smooth transitions respectively. He has been used as a consultant for churches in all auxiliaries to further the work of Christ. Pastor Steve has preached all over the globe to include: Afghanistan, Africa, Czechoslovakia, Honduras, Germany, Pakistan and the United States.

Pastor Steve also served 33 years combined in the US Air Force active duty and reserves.

He can be contacted by email at:
CustomerCare@ForHimMinistries.net